T

# Pregnancy
## THE COMPLETE CHILDBIRTH BOOK

WOLVERHAMPTON CITY LIBRARIES
Withdrawn From Circulation And Sold

........................Received By........................

D1339778

# Pregnancy
## THE COMPLETE CHILDBIRTH BOOK

**NUTAN LAKHANPAL PANDIT**

> **IMPORTANT**
> Please use this book in consultation with your doctor

*Rupa & Co*

This book is dedicated to my
sons Pranav and Akshaya

Also to my aunt Pushpa Sharma,
whose encouragement and blessings have led me
to teach Natural Childbirth Classes.

WOLVERHAMPTON LIBRARIES

W      10.06 N2006

XD000C0CS1163

618.2 PAN

73220

Copyright © Nutan Pandit 2004

First published 1991
Revised Edition 2004
Third Impression 2006

Published by
Rupa & Co
7/16, Ansari Road, Daryaganj,
New Delhi 110002

*Sales Centres:*

Allahabad Bangalore Chandigarh
Chennai Hyderabad Jaipur Kathmandu
Kolkata Mumbai Pune

All rights reserved.
No part of this publication may be reproduced, stored in a
retrieval system, or transmitted, in any form or by any means,
electronic, mechanical, photocopying, recording or otherwise,
without the prior permission of the publishers.

Text illustrations by Priya Nagarajan
Designed by Studio Lynx, Faridabad

Cover photograph by
Mahatta's, New Delhi

Printed in India by
Gopsons Papers Ltd.
A-14, Sector 60 Noida 201 301

# Acknowledgements

I would like to thank Mrs. Merry Wood, the lady from Canada, who taught me breathing practices before my first delivery; the staff of the National Childbirth Trust, London, for permitting me to attend study days, workshops and childbirth classes when I went to London; Dr. Michel Odent, who allowed me to watch how he conducted squatting deliveries, and for showing me his unit replete with facilities for water birth and an operation theatre; Dr. S.K. Bhandari for her encouragement.

I am grateful to Dr. R.L. Bijlani for his invaluable help with my manuscript. Thanks to the following persons for helping me with the completion of my book: Dr. Asha Singh, Dr. Meera Luthra, Dr. Kanwal Hazuria, Dr. Nalini Singh, Dr. Kamla Tiwari, physiotherapist Daulat Dastoor, Dr. Jayant Banerjee, Dr. Prakash Punjabi, Dr. Ratna Zaffar Hussein, Dr. Ashima Abbott, Dr. Preeti Bijlani, Malka Punj, Ashwini Mehta, Sangeeta Gupta, Nita Seth, R. Maniraj, Nirupam Chatterjee, Chitra Sharma and Pradeep Kapoor.

Nutan Lakhanpal Pandit

*For classes in natural childbirth contact:*
Nutan Lakhanpal Pandit,
Natural Childbirth Centre, D-178, Defence Colony, New Delhi 110 024
Tel: 2460 1689, 2469 0552
email: nutanpandit@yahoo.com
website: http://www.ncbchildbirth.com

Ideally contact for classes in the 5th month of pregnancy so that you can attend the course in the 6th month.

# Contents

# Pregnancy Beliefs

**MYTH: The pain is unbearable.**

**F A L S E!** In case of unbearable pain, nature's safety mechanism makes one pass out, i.e. lose consciousness. In labour, women are rendered unconscious by drugs but never by pain. The right attitude to contractions can make it pretty easy to bear.

---

**MYTH: Have a spoon of *ghee* daily to lubricate your nerves.**

**F A L S E!** To make yourself supple, you need exercise, not *ghee*. *Ghee* will make you fat. Be active so that your joints are not rusty and creaky. Earlier, women worked in fields, milked cows, churned butter or ground wheat, hence they could digest the *ghee (see p.77-78)*.

---

**MYTH: The umbilical cord is attached to the mother's navel.**

**F A L S E!** The umbilical cord is attached to an organ inside the womb called the placenta. (The placenta is also called the afterbirth since it is delivered after the baby.) This organ prepares and passes the food and nutrition to the baby, through the umbilical cord, which on the other end, is attached to the baby's navel.

---

**MYTH: Be happy, read good books.**

**T R U E!** If you are afraid or under stress, the chemistry in your body changes as different hormones are released. The baby living within, senses these changes. It is therefore important to strive to be happy.

---

**MYTH: Push when in labour.**

**F A L S E!** When in labour never push until the doctor or the nurse asks you to. If you begin to push when the mouth of the womb is not fully dilated, there is the danger of the baby's head hitting against an unopened cervix (mouth of womb), so that the baby's head and cervix become swollen and tender.

---

**MYTH: Walk when in labour.**

**T R U E!** The best thing you can do is to walk when in labour. Gravity hastens the baby's descent, and therefore shortens labour. Also, when you lie on your back, the weight of your baby and uterus press on a major blood vessel called the vena cava, hence reducing the supply of blood to you and your baby. Less pain is felt when a woman walks in labour. (see page 110)

## MYTH: Eat for two.

**FALSE!** One does not need to eat for two people, but it is important to eat wisely during pregnancy. The baby grows like a parasite, in that, it takes all that it needs, whether the mother has enough or not.
So if you don't eat well, you might end up with a run-down feeling, which comes from the lack of iron in the blood.

## MYTH: If you sit cross legged on the floor it flattens the baby's head.

**FALSE!** The best thing you can do is to sit cross legged, as this exercises the pelvic joints, the very joints that 'open up' when the baby is being born.
With regular exercise, the joints become flexible and open easily at birth. Little wonder sweeper women deliver easily. The baby is safely ensconced in the womb and gets no direct pressure on its head.

## MYTH: Baby gets suffocated if you pull in the stomach.

**FALSE!** The baby does not suffocate, since it gets oxygen through the umbilical cord, which is attached to its navel and to the placenta on the other end. If you pull in your stomach, the weight of the baby is borne by the pelvic bones, so that your stomach muscles get a respite from constant stretching.

## MYTH: Have a glass of milk and *ghee* or have *badam* milk before going to hospital.

**FALSE!** If you have started labour and feel like eating something, eat something light. Once labour has established, if you have something heavy like *badam, ghee*, milk, you'll feel like vomiting (see p. 73-74).

## MYTH: Bind abdomen after delivery.

**F A L S E !** If you make a jumble of your clothes and fling them in the cupboard, they'll fall on your face when you open it next. If you push your muscles back with a girdle, they'll flop out again. It is important instead to do mild exercises for the first forty days or three months and more vigorous ones later to build back tone in your muscles (*see p.159 & 161*).

## MYTH: If the cord is around the neck it is going to be a Caesarean section.

**F A L S E !** Babies are often born with the cord wrapped loosely around their necks. The delivery can be normal.

## MYTH: If the baby is in breech presentation, that is feet first, it will be a Caesarean section.

**F A L S E !** If the baby is breech early in pregnancy, it is likely to turn to a head down position a few weeks before the estimated date of delivery. If it does not turn to a head down position in a woman having her first delivery, a Caesarean will be performed. One month before the estimated date of delivery, homoeopathic medicine taken from a classical* homoeopath could turn around a breech baby. Also accupressure point B67 at the base of the nail of the little toe is known to turn around a breech baby.

* A classical homoeopath is one who asks innumerable questions about how you feel mentally, what illness your parents had, what your likes and dislikes are, etc.

## MYTH: The baby comes on the expected date of delivery.

**F A L S E !** Labour starts on estimated date of delivery in only 4% cases.
One week on either side in 50%, 2 weeks earlier and 1 week later in 80%, at 42 weeks in 10% and at 43 weeks plus in 4% cases.

Source: Text book of Obstetrics by Dr. D.C. Dutta

WOLVERHAMPTON
PUBLIC LIBRARIES

# 1. Birth without Fear

*One truth we gain from living through the years,*
*Fear brings more pain than does the pain it fears.*

John Golden

Childbirth is a natural and universal phenomenon, and yet the knowledge of it among average women is rather haphazard, incomplete, or distorted.

A woman generally has a vague notion that childbirth is unbearable pain and danger. This notion is formed as a result of the distorted tales heard during adolescence or later. What can be pieced together from gossip, movies or fiction draws a picture of passive pain, to which a woman has to submit in utter helplessness. A negative attitude during labour causes her entire body to tense up with fear.

If one undergoes unendurable pain, one passes out as a rule, i.e. loses consciousness. This is nature's safety mechanism. However, women in labour may be rendered unconscious by drugs, but never by pain. Hence, what pain can be felt, can be endured.

## Pain Perception

Pain and childbirth have been associated with each other for so long that normal uterine contractions are often referred to as *pain*.

Uterine contractions and pain have become synonyms. A woman is often told that pain is the signal of labour. In France, labour wards in many units are referred to as the "Hall of Pain". Women who have had babies also talk of "the pain" hence a temporary connection between words and nerve centres takes place.

1

The uterine nerves signal the beginning of labour to the brain. The brain translates it inevitably into pain, anticipating it.

When the human body is healthy and functioning efficiently, the organs constantly send streams of messages to the brain to inform it of their working. Coming from various internal and external sources these messages have to compete with each other. Hence many of them get ignored completely.

However, when the potential force of the brain is reduced, say by shock, we can painfully feel the working of internal organs, e.g. a shocking news can cause a stomachache or a pain in the throat.

In labour, the potential force of the brain can be reduced by a whole lot of negative feedback over a period of time, resulting from the expectation of unbearable pain. In other words, if you expect pain, it can impair the normal activity of the brain, and make you feel greater pain. Each negative feedback regarding labour received over the years has the same effect as drops of water falling regularly at the same spot on a hard stone. Millions of drops do succeed in making a dent.

It is therefore important to think positively about labour. Think of it as a natural experience. As you grow up you experience menstruation, intercourse, and then childbirth. It is a normal and natural function of your body. When labour is allowed to be natural and undrugged, the body releases endorphine hormones that are natural painkillers and give a feeling of well-being.

## The Brain, the Boss

When in labour, the uterus contracts. Stimulus is received and sent to the brain by the nerve endings in the uterus.

2

If the brain interprets it as 'fearful pain' the protective mechanism which advocates flight or fight will take over a woman's body. As a result, the woman, incapable of flight, will fight each contraction by building up muscular tension throughout her body. Along with general muscular rigidity, her uterus will also become rigid and offer resistance to the uterine muscles working towards birth. This is perceived as pain.

However, if the woman understands that the strain her body is undergoing is part of the physical strain associated with the expulsive efforts of her uterus, of which she has no reason to be afraid, the contractions will be a new experience for her. The muscles of her uterus will work unhampered by fearful tension and with each contraction get closer to birth, so that the woman will have a shorter, less painful labour.

Hence the pain a woman will feel in labour will greatly depend on her brain's interpretation of 'pain' as either something fearful or as something to work with.

## Sympathetic Nervous System

When the sympathetic nervous system is stimulated by fear, it restricts the blood flow to and from the uterus. In the absence of adequate fuel and no effective means of disposing of waste products, no organ can function optimally. This is one of the most serious influences of fear on the reproductive organs, and is directly responsible for many of the unpredictable complications of an otherwise normal labour.

According to Langley and Anderson (1893–94), stimulation of the sympathetic nerves to the uterus by fear causes the uterus to appear pallid, firm and

3

bloodless, but when the stimulation is removed, it rapidly fills with blood and becomes an elastic, deep pink uterus. A bloodless, white uterus can lead to urgent distress of the fetus and a Caesarean may have to be performed.

Impairment of circulation is a cause of pain, because the blood flow is too weak to dispose of the by products of metabolism. Restricted circulation can also give rise to severe pain in the muscle tissues of the uterus thereby prolonging the process. Even if the bodily organs are in order, e.g. the pelvis is adequate for the baby's head, and the baby is in the correct position for coming out, psychological fear and its associated pain—not real pain—can make labour long.

Fear and its effects not only prolong labour but are also responsible for haemorrhage and tissue injury in the mother, and anoxaemia (less than normal concentration of oxygen in the blood), respiratory failure, and exhaustion in the newborn infant (see p. 119 & 121).

## Muscle Action

All over the body there are sets of muscles that work in harmony with each other. For example, the muscles in front of and behind the upper arm. Try raising your arm and feel the muscles in front of your upper arm tense. Then lower your arm and feel the muscles in the back of your upper arm tense. Now tense both these muscles together and feel the arm becoming rigid. If the contraction is strong and maintained for some time, the whole arm will quiver and in a short while, there will be considerable pain in the arm.

The same kind of harmonious muscle action is seen in the uterus during childbirth. The uterus is made up of

4

many muscle fibres. One set of muscle fibres are longitudinal, that is, they run from the mouth of the womb, over the front, top and back of the uterus. Contraction of these muscle fibres brings about the expulsion of the baby out of the womb. Then there are circular fibres concentrated in the lower part of the uterus, near its mouth or outlet. The stretching and relaxing of these fibres opens the mouth of the womb. However, if the circular fibres stiffen, they will cause the cervix or mouth of the womb to close and hold up or inhibit the activity of the uterus. This uncalled for rigidity caused by tense muscles can make labour longer and more painful. *(see p. 120)*

# The Body's Design for Birth

A woman's body is designed for giving birth. To begin with, a woman's pelvic

## The female pelvis

There are three joints in the female pelvis that spread apart at birth. Two are at the back, on either side of the sacrum (2), i.e. the lower portion of the backbone where it joins the iliac bones (1) or the basin-like bones of the pelvis. These are called the two sacro–iliac joints. Then there is one joint in front of the pelvis, called the symphysis pubis (3). These three joints spread apart to make way for the baby's exit.

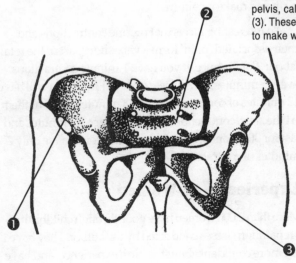

bones are broader than a man's. A woman's pelvis is heart-shaped, whereas a male pelvis is apple-shaped.

After the baby has passed through the cervix or mouth of the uterus, it makes its way through the vagina. The vagina is made up of folds and is therefore capable of unfolding, just as the pleats in front of a saree can unfold. As the baby passes through the vagina, it opens up to make way for the baby. The more relaxed a woman keeps the muscles of the vaginal passage, the less tension the baby's head encounters during birth.

The cranial or head bones of the baby are not fused. As the baby's head negotiates the birth canal, these bones can mould to the size of the vaginal passage. They can also override each other if necessary. At birth the bones come back to their original shape. It is because of this that some babies are born with funny bumps on their heads, which smooth out in a few days.

The body releases hormones to control the process of birth and make it pain-free.

An interesting fact is that uterine contractions and their associated 'pain' form a very short part of the total labour. For instance, if you have 1-minute contractions every 5 minutes, it will mean that in 1 hour you will have 12 minutes of contractions and 48 minutes without them. At the start, contractions could be every 15 minutes and last for 30 seconds. So in 1 hour, one would have only 2 minutes of contractions.

## Experience of Women

More than 2,000 women have gone through childbirth preparation classes conducted by the author. They have felt more confident about the birth experience, and have gone through it with little or no pain.

A psychologically prepared woman can handle any kind of labour confidently. Says Rita, who had a Caesarean section: 'Around 4.30 a.m. there was a heavy flow of blood as the placenta had started separating from the uterine wall. It was accidental haemorrhage. By the time I was operated two-thirds of the placenta had separated and there was foetal distress. The best thing about my delivery was my cute baby girl whose life and mine were saved by timely treatment administered to me by my efficient doctor, as my case had become very serious.'

When a woman understands that in her case a Caesarean section is necessary, she accepts the decision consciously. Moreover, since she has been handling her labour with breathing and relaxation, she is in good mental and physical health. Since she is calm and collected, she will let the anesthetist send her to sleep with a greatly reduced amount of anesthesia, so that both she and her baby will experience less discomfort afterwards. At the same time, when women become knowledgeable, they will not accept anything blindly.

When a woman has not prepared herself at all for giving birth, and she fears it, she may be filled with a dread of labour. Each contraction will become a signal of pain and therefore pain will result. On the other hand, a trained woman can have a very positive attitude towards birth and may have a smooth and easy labour.

There is one category of women who fail to make progress once labour begins. Throughout pregnancy they display no anxiety and appear to be happy. But once labour begins, they lose heart, and begin

One must have positive feelings – that's what counts. You can face anything.

NEHA BALI
Computer based training developer

I tried to help her by reminding her and helping her to concentrate and breathe.

VIVEK BALI
Neha's husband

Found that the breathing and relaxation helped tremendously. Thanks to the classes and exercises, I did not feel at all apprehensive and on the whole found labour not difficult to bear.

RUKSHANA SHROFF

complaining that nothing is happening and often end up with slow progress, long labour, and may be a Caesarean. Such a woman is one who suppresses her innate fears and leaves them buried in her subconscious mind, only for them to surface at the time of labour, hampering the normal sequence of events.

In Dr. Dick Read's book, *Childbirth Without Fear*, a case is mentioned that illustrates this point. There was a physio-therapist who had been 'a very keen exponent of relaxation and preparation for childbirth'. She had a very easy and trouble–free first labour, with minimum discomfort. When she had her second baby, she suddenly experienced very strong contractions. They were so strong that she immediately suspected that something was wrong. She suddenly 'lost her nerve and literally began to scream the place down.' She was immediately given inhalation analgesia and brought under control, and the baby was born normally. She later admitted that she had expected her second labour to be easier than her first, and when she had felt more discomfort than expected, she had thought the worst and lost control of herself, so that fear took over. In the labour following her second one, she had a comparatively easy time again, since the circumstances of her fear had been explained to her. She understood that no two labours were alike, and that sometimes in second and subsequent labours strong contractions are experienced.

Fears repressed into the background can lead to problems during birth. So it is important for every pregnant woman to come out with her fears or imaginings, to discuss them with the doctor, and understand them. No two labours are alike; each is different. Even in one woman, two labours will not be

> Labour was absolutely wonderful. I knew exactly what to expect – the breathing was great – otherwise my mom had said she would not be able to see me through the labour pains. Breathing helped me so much that it was almost painless.
>
> AMRITA KHOSLA
> second delivery
> (first by
> Caesarean)

> Like a Buddha she would sit up and mumble something each time a contraction came – I thought she was muttering her mantra but she said it was her breathing.
>
> VANDANA
> JAGWANI'S
> MOTHER

8

alike. Divest yourself of any preconceived notions about labour. There is no right or wrong, perfect or imperfect in labour. Your labour just happens, you cannot set specific goals for it. You simply equip yourself with some knowledge and relaxation and breathing techniques.

## Natural Childbirth

Natural childbirth implies having one's baby the natural way, that is, in a relaxed attitude, without anesthesia or analgesics and without any mechanical aid to birth.

An interesting description of a woman in labour is given in Dr. Dick Read's book *Childbirth Without Fear*, London, 1977, which influenced Dr. Read to such an extent that he became a pioneer of natural birth in Britain.

He describes the incident thus: 'In due course the baby was born. There was no fuss or noise. Everything seemed to have been carried out according to an ordered plan. There was only one slight dissension: I tried to persuade my patient to let me put the mask over her face and give her some chloroform when the head appeared and dilation of the passage was obvious. She, however, resented the suggestion and firmly but kindly refused to take this help.

It was the first time in my short experience that I had ever been refused when offering chloroform. I asked her why she would not use the mask. She looked from the old woman who had been assisting, to the window through which was bursting the first light of dawn and then shyly turned to me and said: "It didn't hurt. It wasn't meant to, was it, doctor?" I began to realise that there was no law in nature and no design that could justify the pain of childbirth.'

# 2. Your Anatomy

It is important for every woman to understand the anatomy of her body. To do so a woman should freely feel and examine her body. Do not be shy of your body. Most women are not familiar with the appearance of their sexual organs as compared to the other parts of their body. Women tend to consider themselves unclean "down there" and have as little to do with the area as possible. It is good to know that the vagina, which has a natural self-cleansing process, is cleaner than the inside of the mouth. Feel good about your body, it is not unclean or obscene. It is you. Get familiar with yourself. You are unique in your ability to reproduce. Each month your periods reaffirm your fertility. Take a mirror and have a look at yourself "down there". Lie down on the bed, bend legs at knees. Place feet flat on bed, move thighs apart and hold a mirror between them. In a mature woman the single most obvious feature will be the pubic hair.

If you look lower down from the pubis, which is the fatty hair-covered mass just below the lower abdomen, you will notice your sexual as well as your excretory organs. You will notice an area shaped like an inverted V, within the outer hairy flaps. The two arms of the V are the lips of the vagina. The tip of the V, which is on top instead of down, has in it the clitoris and the hood of clitoris, which is the most sensitive spot in the area. The clitoris becomes erect during sexual arousal, just as the penis becomes erect during sexual arousal in a man. Within the lips of the vagina, and below the clitoris, there are two openings or orifices. The small opening just below the clitoris is the urethra from where urine

1. Pubic hair
2. Clitoris
3. Urinary Opening
4. Vaginal Opening
5. Anus
6. Perineum

10

is passed. Below the urethra is a larger opening, the vagina. Your vagina is the opening through which the menstrual flow passes, and through which your baby will be born. It is made up of folds which afford it elasticity. These unfold when the vagina expands during intercourse or childbirth. Below the vagina, further back, is the anus. Through the anus stool is passed. The urethra leads up to the bladder, a bag in which urine collects before urination. The anus leads up to the rectum, the last part of the large intestine where faecal matter collects before being expelled as stool.

1. Rectum
2. Uterus
3. Bladder
4. Cervix
5. Urinary opening
6. Vaginal opening
7. Anus

   The uterus is the organ that is going to carry your baby when you get pregnant. It has thick walls and lies between the bladder and the rectum. It may be folded backwards or forwards slightly, in which case it is called retroverted or anteverted respectively. It corrects itself in pregnancy and will not cause complications at birth. Its upper part is called its body, and the lower, narrower part is called the cervix or mouth of the womb. If you wash your hands and insert a finger in your vagina, you can touch your cervix since it protrudes into the vagina. It feels like a dimpled nose tip or like a chin. The entrance into the uterus through the cervix is very small and is called the os.

The top part of the uterus has two openings on either side that lead to a fine tube on either side, called fallopian tubes. The other end of the tube is funnel-shaped and leads to the ovaries on either side. The ovaries are two in number and the size of an unshelled almond. They are placed on either side of the uterus. The ovaries have 2 functions. They produce the female sex hormones oestrogen and progestrone. They also produce the ovum or egg which is wafted into the fallopian tube on being released. It is then fertilised by the sperm, which travels

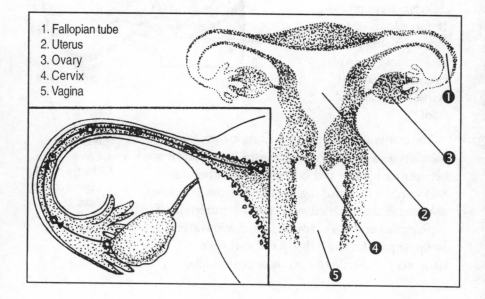

1. Fallopian tube
2. Uterus
3. Ovary
4. Cervix
5. Vagina

from the vagina, through the cervix, into the uterus, and from the uterus to the fallopian tube.

The fertilised egg then journeys back to the uterus from the fallopian tube and houses itself in the body of the uterus, where it begins to grow. As the fertilised egg grows, the thick walls of the uterus thin out as it enlarges and balloons up with the pregnancy. In rare instances the fertilised ovum implants itself not in the wall of the uterus, but in the fallopian tube, and very rarely in the abdominal cavity, on the ovary, or the cervix. Such a pregnancy is called an ectopic pregnancy and surgery is normally required to end it. Signs of ectopic pregnancy are sharp abdominal pain. Pain due to ectopic pregnancy is aggravated by body motion, such as bending over, rising or travelling in a car. Discomfort connected with ectopic pregnancy usually occurs in the first 3 months of pregnancy.

## The Development of the Baby

It can be divided into three specific periods of 3 months each, together making 9 months.

By the end of the first 3 months the baby is about 3½ inches long. The vital organs and limbs are fully formed but not sufficiently developed. The amniotic sac contains about 3.5 ounces of amniotic fluid and the fetus has plenty of room to move about, although the movements will not yet be felt by the mother. The heart is beating, the eyes, though closed, are in position. The facial features are properly formed and the ears are in place on the sides of the head. The sex organs are developed so that the baby has a male or female identity.

*The first trimester: 1–3 months*

13

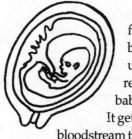

The fetus swallows the amniotic fluid, most of which is used by its body, and it produces drops of sterile urine. The amniotic fluid is constantly refreshed by the amniotic sac. As the baby is not breathing, it does not choke. It gets its oxygen from the mother's bloodstream through the umbilical cord.

## The second trimester: 4–6 months

By the end of the second trimester the baby is about 14 inches long, roughly the length of his mother's fist and forearm, and weighs about 1 kilogram.

At the start of the second trimester, or from the 4th month onwards, the mother begins to feel movements of the fetus, and she begins 'to show'.
The fetus can now smile and suck its thumb. At the ends of the fingers and toes, ridges develop, giving the baby a unique identity of fingerprints.

The trunk and legs of the fetus lengthen and the head no longer looks too large for the rest of its body. Eyelashes and eyebrows appear, although the eyes remain closed until the end of this trimester.

The skin begins to grow a coat of fine downy hair called lanugo, which is shed before or shortly after birth. During this period the baby also develops a whitish greasy coating called vernix from the oil secreted from its skin and dead skin cells.

The fetus now swallows a pint of amniotic fluid daily and returns it to the amniotic sac through urination. The amniotic fluid is recycled every hour, when one-third of it is absorbed into the

14

mother's bloodstream and replaced with fresh fluid secreted from the amniotic sac.

During the last 3 months the baby gains weight, and slowly grows to reach right up to the mother's breastbone. As the fetus becomes large it can no longer move freely as before, since it gets cramped for space. So now instead of movements of the fetus, the mother feels its kicks and pokes.

*The third trimester: 7–9 months*

During this trimester the baby stores up protein to build muscles, calcium for its bones, iron for its red blood cells, fat to insulate it against changes in temperature after birth.

By the end of the 7th month the fetus' brain matures to be able to cope with

**1. Uterus/womb**
A muscular organ in which the baby lives until birth.

**2. Placenta/afterbirth**
A tissue growth on the inside of the uterus. It is delivered after the birth of the baby, after its need and function are over; hence the name *afterbirth*. The placenta matures towards the end of pregnancy.

**3. Umbilical Cord**
A rope of blood vessels attached to the baby at its navel on one end and to the placenta on the other. Through it nutrients reach the baby.

**4. Amniotic Sac/Bag of Water**
A membrane sac filled with liquid called amniotic fluid, in which the baby floats, and which acts as a shock absorber, protecting the baby in case of accidental knocks.

**5. Cervix**
The mouth of the uterus, leading to the birth canal. The baby passes through the muscular opening at the cervix and then through the birth canal to the outside world.

**6. Mucus Plug**
A plug of mucus and blood, that plugs up the cervix much as a cork plugs up a bottle. It prevents infection from entering the womb.

breathing and swallowing. Thumb sucking is now resorted to more frequently. If born at this stage the baby has a 90% chance of surviving.

By the end of the 8th month the fetus looks quite like what it will at birth. Although the lungs are not yet fully operational, the baby has a 95% chance of surviving if born at this stage.

It is during the last trimester that the fetus' eyes open. The senses undergo their greatest development at this stage. The hair on the head grow and fingernails and toenails develop.

Sometime during the 9th month the fetus generally turns head down in the womb. About 2 weeks before birth, it descends about 2 inches, settling in the mother's pelvic bones. This is called lightening, engagement, fixing, or, dropping of the head.

The mother feels lighter as the pressure of the fetus pushing on her diaphragm and lungs is reduced, so that she can breathe more easily. Mild contractions of the muscles of the womb may be felt in the 9th month as the womb changes the baby into the head down position or as the womb prepares its muscles for delivery. Some times babies are born feet first. Such babies are called breech babies.

# 3. Pregnancy

The simplest way of knowing that you are pregnant is the missed period. Along with a missed period a woman may feel nauseous, may need to urinate more frequently and feel tenderness in the breasts. When you go to the doctor in order to reconfirm your pregnancy, the doctor will check you for an enlarged uterus, softening of genital organs and during an internal vaginal examination the cervix will be seen to have taken on a purplish-velvety look, typical of pregnancy.

## Blood / Urine Test

A blood or urine test can help detect the presence of a pregnancy. The blood or urine is tested for the presence of HCG, human chorionic gonadotropin. The developing placenta begins to produce this hormone to prevent menstruation and protect the pregnancy. For an earlier result the blood test is more reliable.

High dose hormone tablets used to be given earlier to test pregnancy. It would make the period occur if there was no pregnancy. If there was a pregnancy and if the fetus was female there was a possibility that the tablet could produce masculinisation. Tablets are not used to test for pregnancy anymore. Instead, tablets with a different hormonal combination are now used to abort an unwanted pregnancy. If tests or a visit to the doctor confirm that you are pregnant, you must immediately start taking care of yourself and your baby by eating nutritious food, avoiding too much tea, coffee, and colas, stopping alcohol, tobacco, and indiscriminate use of medicines and tranquillisers.

When you visit your dentist or general physician tell him that you are pregnant, because medicines of

17

all kinds should be avoided, particularly in the first 3 months of pregnancy. The thalidomide tragedy in 1962 jolted people into realising that drugs taken by the mother affect not only her but also the baby. Thalidomide was a sedative prescribed to women in early pregnancy. Over 5000 children throughout the world were born with limb defects, in some cases with no limbs at all. Drugs that affect the rapidly developing fetus in the first 12 weeks are called teratogenic. As Dr. Gordon Bourne says in *Pregnancy*, 'Teratogenic drugs should not be given at any stage of pregnancy. These include thalidomide, phenytoin, anti-thyroid drugs, anti-cancer agents, some sex hormones, alcohol, tetracycline and some anesthetic agents.' Only a doctor will be able to tell the correct dose of a drug, should it need to be used. If you are a patient of diabetes or epilepsy you must not stop your medication without consulting your doctor. Any medicine should be taken strictly under the doctor's supervision, even if it is only an aspirin.

Many ancient cultures like the Indian, Japanese and Chinese stress that the mood and activities of a pregnant woman should be positive and happy, since they believe that what the mother is exposed to in pregnancy affects the growing baby within her. Hippocrates tells of his belief that a pregnant woman directly influences the baby she carries.

According to a legend, when Confucius' mother became pregnant, she withdrew to a mountain to pray and gave birth to Confucius there. In ancient China a pregnant woman was told not to look at ugly things, not to listen to rude talk, not to speak about trivial matters and not to listen to gossip.

Take time off to relax *(see p.96)*. Researchers have recently inserted small microphones into the uterus and recorded what the fetus hears. The womb, they find, is full of the mother's bodily music; the whooshing bowels, the gurgling stomach and, the mother's heart beat.

Dr. Lee Salk, a leading psychologist, in his classic experiment took 2 groups of infants. One group was exposed to a recording of the human heart beat of 80 per minute. The second group was unexposed. After four days the group exposed to the sound of the beating heart had gained more weight on an average, as compared to the unexposed group. In the second test he played a recording of a heart beating at 120 beats per minute, a typical rate achieved in an anxious or frightened adult. The rapid rate was so distressing to the newborn babies that the experiment had to be terminated at once. Little wonder that mothers the world over hold the baby close to their breast to comfort it. It could be that the baby is soothed quickly in this position because it hears the familiar pulsation of the heart that it did in the womb.

## Planning a Healthy Baby

Today, with the means of contraception easily available and the number of working women on the increase, a pregnancy is often planned and not accidental. If you are a diabetic, your condition will need to be assessed before your pregnancy to avoid complications later:

To conceive, all contraception should be stopped. If you are on the pill, you should go off it, and switch to the condom and spermicidal pessaries for 2 to 3 months, so that all hormones are out of your system by the time you conceive. Biologically it is best to have your baby in your 20s. Risks increase in the under 20s and over 40s, and slightly in the over 30s.

# Genetic Counselling

If there is a history of epilepsy or severe myopia in your or your husband's family, you may like to consult a genetic counsellor. Genetic counselling is a way of discovering whether your child may be born with an inherited disorder. It is available in most large hospitals. The counsellor will ask about your and your husband's family history. A blood test may be done to get more information. If there is a problem, the counsellor will help you find out if you may pass it on. You will also be told if tests that can detect the disorder in the fetus during pregnancy are available.

*Using knees and legs for lifting*

**Step 1**
Standing close to a child or object, put one foot forward and drop to one knee.

# Pre-Conception Care

A few months before you plan to conceive, have a blood test taken to check if you are anaemic. If you get your anaemia under control, it will go a long way towards producing a healthy baby. So eat foods rich in iron *(see p. 64)*. Eating wisely is important both for you and your husband. A nutritious diet, less stress, less alcohol and cigarettes, less lead exhaust from vehicles, less caffeine from tea, coffee and cola drinks, no indiscriminate use of drugs, are all factors that will contribute to a strong and healthy baby. If you and your husband can check these factors before you conceive, it should give a strong foundation to your baby. You should check these factors 3 to 6 months before conception, especially approximately 15 days before the next period is expected, because the

**Step 2**
Rise to your feet keeping your back straight and lifting with the front leg while the back foot balances.

pregnancy starts at that time. Always check these factors throughout pregnancy. A man's diet, smoking and drinking habits, etc., can harm his sperms. It is being increasingly proved that health and nutritional status of both the man and the woman before conception is very important.

A couple which takes care of all these factors have done their best to produce a healthy baby. It may require a slight alteration of lifestyle, but it will give you a healthier baby and mother. A healthier mother will be able to cope more easily with the care of the baby later.

During pregnancy keep up your normal activities but do not overwork. Avoid lifting heavy things, as it can lead to a miscarriage. Regular exercise will help you keep fit (see p. 81). Normal activities will help keep your muscles toned up, making your delivery easy.

## Antenatal Visits

When you become pregnant, you must consult an obstetrician or an Obstetrics OPD in a hospital or a medical centre. Often 3 months pass by the time a woman goes for consultation. Under medical guidance you will go through pregnancy and birth with fewer complications. Any potentially dangerous situation will be controlled through preventive measures. For instance, a woman with a Rhesus-negative blood group will be given an anti-D immunoglobin injection after the birth of her first baby so that her second delivery will be problem free. A Rhesus-negative woman, who has not had an anti-D injection after her first delivery or after an abortion preceding her first delivery, may have a baby that will need a complete blood transfusion at birth. (see p. 60)

A woman with swollen feet, hands and face will also need to follow simple medical advice so that other complications do not crop up. Blood pressure and weight will also be checked at antenatal visits.

The doctor will ask about your previous

pregnancies, miscarriages, abortions, about when you had your last period, what contraception you have been using, what illnesses you have suffered from, etc.

Until the 7th month you will be called for a checkup once a month. Until the 9th month you will be called every 15 days and then every week until you go into labour. The doctor will prescribe certain tests.

# Blood Tests during Pregnancy

A blood test will be taken to find out the haemoglobin content of the blood. Haemoglobin is the red colouring matter of the blood that carries life-giving oxygen to all parts of the mother's body, including the baby. Haemoglobin levels tend to fall in pregnancy and could drop to as low as 9.5gms/100ml (see p.58-59)

Your blood group will also be noted, in case you need a blood transfusion in an emergency. The blood will be checked to see if it is Rhesus-negative or Rhesus-positive (see p. 60). A blood test, **Hbs Ag** is also recommended sometimes to test for hepatitis.

*VDRL*
*Venereal*
*Disease*
*Research Lab*
*test*

The Venereal Disease Research Lab test is a blood test that checks for the presence of any sexually transmitted disease or venereal disease. If, for instance, a woman is found to have syphilis, she can give birth to a deformed child. Both the woman and her husband should have the VDRL test. Even if it turns out that one of them has the disease, both will receive a course of antibiotic injections to protect themselves and the baby. It is important that both partners cooperate with the doctor.

There may be other instances when the doctor would prescribe a blood test. Medical supervision is therefore essential.

---

The Alpha-Feto-Protein test is a specialised blood test that can reveal if there are any major defects in the baby. The mother's blood is checked for alpha-feto-protein which is a protein that is produced by the baby's liver and is passed to the mother's bloodstream through the placenta. It is most accurate between 16 and 18 weeks of pregnancy. If the test suggests that the baby is not normal, it should be repeated. If the second test gives similar results the fetus also should be checked by an ultrasound scan and amniocentesis.

*AFP*
*Alpha-Feto-Protein test*

---

A comprehensive blood test called TORCH tests the blood for various infections like toxoplasma, syphilis, rubella or german measles, cytomegalo-virus, and herpes or Hepatitis B.

*TORCH*

When these infections are found present they may manifest in the child in the months following birth. If they are already present then their treatment can begin at birth. For instance, immunisation against Hepatitis B can be given to the baby in the weeks following birth if the infection is present in the mother. Likewise, treatment for toxoplasma infection or syphilis infection can be started at birth. In other words, prior knowledge of any infection can make it possible for an early diagnosis and appropriate medical care for the child.

---

**Toxoplasmosis** is a parasitic infection that can be acquired from soil, cat faeces and raw meat.

*Pets, Gardening, Raw Meat (Toxoplasma)*

23

It is an infection present in birds and animals. It is also a common dormant infection in humans. Its presence in humans varies from population to population, but it is more prevalent in warmer, more humid climates.

A woman who has already been infected by it before becoming pregnant, will be immune to it. Her baby will not be threatened by it. It is only when a woman acquires this infection in her pregnancy, that the baby could be affected by it. Approximately 50% of women who acquire this infection and are not treated can pass it to the baby. However, if this infection is identified and treated with antibodies (spiramycin for instance) it reduces the risk of damage by 50% to 60%. Infection can result mainly in abnormalities of the brain and growth retardation.

The damage caused by this infection is the greatest in mothers who acquire this infection in the first three months of pregnancy. (Interestingly the incidence of transmission of infection to the baby is least in early pregnancy, and greatest in late pregnancy.)

To prevent this infection a woman can follow simple guidelines. She should eat only well cooked meat and eggs, and drink only pasteurised milk or boiled milk. Avoid handling raw meat. If handling raw meat, the hands should be washed immediately, and kitchen surfaces and vessels washed well thereafter. Do not touch mouth or eyes while handling raw meat. Wash fruits and vegetables before consumption. Protect food from flies and cockroaches. When gardening or handling faeces of animals use gloves.

## HIV/AIDS

A blood test, tests for the Human Immunodeficiency Virus. A person who tests positive for HIV has a

24

strong possibility of developing AIDS (Acquired Immuno-Deficiency Syndrome), in which case a person's immunity or strength to fight infection falls drastically so that the person picks up all kinds of infections like cold, respiratory and skin infections, etc. If a woman is suffering from AIDS she can pass the infection to her new born baby.

The time of transmission of infection to the baby could be within the womb or at the time of birth. Breast milk can also transmit the infection. A child born to an HIV infected mother should have regular investigative tests until the age of 6 to 8 months to check if the child has got the infection from the mother or not. If the mother has HIV infection, pregnancy can increase her chance of developing AIDS.

However if a woman is known to be HIV or AIDS infected and gets pregnant, recent research has shown that the use of two standard drugs **azt** and **3tc** can block the passing of the virus from the mother to the baby. Recent research also shows that without treatment 17% of babies can be infected, whereas with treatment the infection of babies can be lowered to 11% percent if the two drugs are given when labour begins, and continued for a week after birth. The medicine can be given to the mother when labour starts and it must be given to both mother and child for a week following birth. This is to protect the child from exposure to HIV contaminated blood and secretions as well as from virus in the breast milk, which causes $1/3$rd of all infections in the young.

The risk of infection can be further reduced to 9% if treatment is begun 26 weeks before delivery and continued for a week afterwards.

A new drug, **Nevirapine** is also known to reduce

the transmission of HIV from mother to baby, and costs much less than azt. Nevirapine is administered to an HIV infected woman in labour, and another dose is given to the baby within 3 days of birth.

## Urine Test

A urine test is routine in pregnancy. The urine will be analysed for infection, and for glucose which will show up if there is diabetes. Ketones may show up if you are vomiting a lot or not eating enough. In late pregnancy albumin or protein in the urine will indicate pre-eclampsia (see p. 57).

## Internal Vaginal Examination

An internal examination could be done at the start of pregnancy and at its end, and sometimes during its course. At the start of pregnancy it could be done to confirm the pregnancy and exclude any possibility of abnormalities of the pelvis, vagina, or cervix.

At the end of pregnancy it could be done to check the readiness of the cervix or its ripeness. It does not harm the baby. It will help if you breathe out slowly through the mouth while it is being carried out, and relax your pelvic floor as you do when passing urine.

## Abdominal Examination

When you go for a checkup the size and shape of your abdomen will be felt by the doctor after making you lie down. The doctor will examine your abdomen for its shape and size, for abdominal scars and for the

26

movements of the fetus. By palpating your abdomen with one or both hands the doctor can gain a lot of information about the size of the baby, in what position the baby is lying and the presentation of its head.

The height of the growing uterus also gives an idea of the growth of the baby. At 3 months the uterus can be felt in the lower abdomen, rising out of the pelvis. At 5½ the uterus reaches the height of the navel. At 7½ months the uterus will be halfway between the navel and the breastbone, or the region below the breasts. In the 9th month the uterus will reach the area below the breasts.

## Ultrasound

Ultrasound was first used during the Second World War to detect submarines. In a pregnant woman, sound waves are directed to the fetus inside the uterus, and as they bounce off the baby's bones and tissues, a picture of the fetus appears on a TV screen. The picture may not make much sense to you, but the expert working the machine will be able to interpret it. It is really quite simple. Even a novice would be able to differentiate the dark areas, which are fluid-filled, from the white areas which are solid.

When you go for an ultrasound scan, you must have a full bladder. You will be made to lie down next to the machine and an oily substance will be spread over your abdomen. A small flat device will be moved slowly all over your abdomen during the scan.

It is a fairly new technology that has begun to be widely used in obstetrics in India only from the early 1980s. In other words, it is in its infancy. It does not appear to harm the mother or the baby in any way but there is no evidence that it is completely safe either. It took 40 years to discover the harmful effects of X-ray,

27

which was the only technique of getting some information of the baby in the uterus before the ultrasound scan.

As a diagnostic tool the ultrasound is invaluable, since it can give the doctor vital information on diagnosis of pregnancy, missed abortion, hydatidiform mole, ectopic pregnancies, twin pregnancies, the position of the fetus and placenta, the age of the fetus, abnormalities of the fetus or uterus. Scans should be done in pregnancy if the doctor thinks it advisable for investigative purposes. As a routine procedure it is avoidable.

According to Maye's *Midwifery* (1997) 'An Ultrasound scan is usually performed between 16 and 18 weeks gestation, and maybe repeated later in pregnancy if indicated.' An ultrasound done between 16 to 20 weeks gives an accurate idea of how old the pregnancy is. After 24 weeks, the baby's age in the uterus cannot be accurately predicted by an ultrasound.

Dr. Ian Donald, professor of obstetrics from Glasgow who pioneered the use of ultrasound in obstetrics*, wrote 40 years later: 'Perhaps the time has now come to stand and stare and to take stock of where we are going...bearing in mind that sonar** must never lose its submissiveness to the medical art and the paramount importance of the patient...viewed with a sense of proportion sonar comes as a commodity only, though with many uses. Out of control, it can be an obsession, a tail that wags the dog...sonar is not a new medical religion...nor an end in itself. A tool exploited for its own sake is no better than a saw given to a small boy for cutting wood, who must presently look around the house for suitable objects of

* a branch of medical science concerned with pregnancy and childbirth

** ultrasound

28

furniture inviting amputation...the possibility of hazard should be kept under constant review.' *(Source: Association of Improvement in Maternity Services-AIMS-U.K.,1994)*

# Amniocentesis

This is a procedure where a small amount of fluid is taken out from the pregnant mother's abdomen (amniotic sac) to test for chromosomal and other abnormalities. It is not a routine test. Under local anesthesia a needle is inserted into the mother's abdomen and a little bit of amniotic fluid is withdrawn. This is done along with an ultrasound, so that the placenta and the fetus are not disturbed by the needle. The fluid which contains fetal cells can then be analysed for the detection of abnormalities of the nervous system, mental handicaps, including Mongolism or Down's Syndrome, inherited disorders, etc.

Even though it might be carried out efficiently under hygienic conditions, there is a 1–2 % chance that it might lead to a spontaneous abortion. Besides, the couple should first decide what they want to do with the results of the test. If the tests suggest an abnormality, are they ready to opt for termination of the pregnancy? This can be difficult, for the test cannot be done before 14 weeks of pregnancy, when a termination would mean having an induced labour. If a woman already has one abnormal child, she might want to consider this test. She should seek the advice of her

29

doctor.

## Anti-Tetanus Injection

Anti-tetanus injections are given routinely to all pregnant women. An anti-tetanus injection taken by the mother in pregnancy protects both the mother and the baby from tetanus infection for up to several months after the birth. It is usually given in 2 doses in the 26th week and 6 weeks later.

## Medical Termination of Pregnancy

Amniocentesis or the AFP test may suggest the baby has a severe abnormality of the spine or brain. If you catch an infection of German measles or rubella in the first 3 months of pregnancy, it can physically and mentally handicap the child. Chickenpox can do similar things. In such cases the doctor would advise an abortion. It is better to go for an abortion than to live with an abnormal child for the rest of your life with a guilty feeling that you could have avoided all this pain to yourself and your baby. Discuss things with your doctor and if you like, with a psychotherapist as well.

Medical termination of pregnancy is now easily available and quite safe. It is offered by voluntary organisations like the Marie Stopes Clinic, public hospitals and private clinics. It should not be resorted to as a contraceptive method, in which case repeated abortions can seriously harm a woman's health.

## Boy or Girl ?

When the ovum is fertilised by the male sperm, 23 chromosomes each are contributed by the male and the female, making a total of 46 chromosomes. Of the sex chromosomes, one is contributed by the male and the other by the female. These are the famous XX (girl) chromosome present in the female and the XY (boy) chromosome present in the male. The mother always contributes the X chromosome. The sex of the child is determined by the father's contribution of the sex chromosome. If it is X the baby born will be female. If it is Y the baby born will be male.

There are some not very scientific theories that claim to be able to tilt the balance towards the conception of a male or female child, as desired. One such theory propounded by a French doctor, François Papa, claims that if a woman follows a particular kind of diet for 2 to 3 months before conception, she can choose a male or female baby. This diet is discussed at length in the book *Boy or Girl: Choosing Your Child Through Your Diet*. (Ritana Books, New Delhi)

Some doctors in Canada and France have been advocating the diet theory and say it has an 80% chance of success. For a girl, they advise a diet rich in starch, milk and milk products, and low in salt. They also recommend taking a tablet of calcium every day. For a boy, they advise eating a high salt diet, with plenty of meat and fruit. Milk and milk products are not permitted. A daily potassium tablet may also be recommended.

According to *The Complete Handbook of Pregnancy* edited by W. Rose–Neil, research studies have shown that the more often you have intercourse, the more likely you are to have a boy. More boys tend to be born, for example, in the first few years after marriage, immediately following a reunion after a long parting, and in younger parents.

The timing of intercourse is also said to influence the

sex of the child. If conception takes place within 48 hours after ovulation you are more likely to have a male child. Within 48 hours of ovulation, intercourse should take place at least 3 times, and then one should refrain until the next period. The opposite would apply to conceive a female child. That is, intercourse should take place 48 hours after ovulation to conceive a female child. In order to pinpoint the exact time of ovulation, ultrasound clinics offer a package deal. You are called for an ultrasound every day, 3 days after your period is over. You have to go early in the morning on a full bladder. You go until ultrasound detects that ovulation has taken place.

Another way to pinpoint ovulation would be the temperature method (see p.170).

Douching is also said to influence the sex of the child. An alkaline vaginal douche before intercourse is said to help conceive a boy. An alkaline vaginal douche can be made of 1 tablespoon bicarbonate of soda dissolved in 500 ml of warm distilled water. To conceive a girl, an acid douche can be made from 1 tablespoon of white vinegar and 1 tablespoon of warm distilled water. If you are very keen on conceiving either a daughter or a son you could discuss these methods with your doctor.

# 4. Common Problems in Pregnancy

Most of the common ailments during pregnancy are minor and can be relieved by simple changes in lifestyle. As a result of tremendous changes occurring in the body, discomfort, muscle pulls, bleeding gums and cramps, are some of the accepted problems a pregnant woman is likely to encounter. However, some lucky women never face any problem at all. Consult your doctor if you are in doubt about your symptoms.

## Physical Changes

**Darkening pigmentation**

With pregnancy it is common to develop a darkening of certain areas of the body, like the darkening of the nipple and areola; or the darkening of a line starting from below the navel and ending at the pubic hair; or the development of dark patches on the face.

These are caused by pregnancy hormones. These hormones tend to make skin cells containing dark pigment enlarge, so that any birth mark, freckles, moles or scars tend to become darker after the 3rd month of pregnancy.

These changes mostly disappear after birth, but in some cases they remain. These are normal accompaniments of pregnancy and therefore no cause for worry.

**Breast changes**

Breasts often become tender and sensitive to touch in early pregnancy. The tenderness passes by middle pregnancy.

The dark area around the nipple, the areola, gets darker. This is a permanent change in most women.

33

Stretch marks on the breasts may occur in women with large, heavy or sagging breasts. Hence, in case of a dramatic increase in breast size, you must wear a well-fitting cotton bra, that supports the weight of the breasts. (A nylon bra tends to sag with the weight.) This will not only prevent stretch marks, but prevent sagging too.

---

These are dark, swollen veins that might appear on the legs during pregnancy, and sometimes remain forever afterwards.

*Varicose veins*

The veins in the legs do the job of carrying impure blood back to the heart for purification. In some women the veins become lax or weak during pregnancy. Due to this laxity they cannot push back the blood through the congested pelvic area, so that the blood tends to pool in the legs, causing the appearance of varicose veins.

To prevent their appearance, avoid standing for long periods without moving. Do not cross your legs when sitting on a chair, since this reduces circulation in the legs. Put your feet up on a stool whenever possible. At least once in the day, place your legs higher than your hips. Sit on a chair, put your feet on the table. Or, lying down on the floor, place your feet on a stool, low chair or bed. When sitting for long periods, like at a desk for instance, write alphabets, A,B,C etc. with your toes in the air.

> **PRECAUTION**
> *Do not point toes if prone to leg cramps. (see p.36)*

## Teeth and gums

During pregnancy the gums soften and are therefore more likely to catch infection and start bleeding. Infection in the gums can mean infection in the teeth also, and consequent tooth decay.

Plaque is a layer of bacteria that grows on gums and teeth. Bacteria in plaque thrive on the pieces of food stuck between the teeth, and feed on sugar. If you eat a lot of sugary foods, you increase the amount of plaque in your mouth. If you eat less sugar, the bacteria will not get such a good chance to grow and multiply.

Plaque left on the teeth can eat into the enamel, which is the surface of the tooth. If this is continued, the tooth will keep on decaying until it affects the nerve inside, in the centre of the tooth, causing a toothache.

In order that plaque does not get a chance to form, it is important to brush your teeth regularly and to keep your mouth clean. The good old Indian habit of swishing the mouth a few times with fresh water after a meal is good. That apart, brush before sleeping. The best thing is to brush after every meal.

In pregnancy your gums and teeth are in a more delicate condition, so a soft brush is preferred to a hard one. A brush with a small head will reach all the corners and surfaces of your teeth more easily. Change your toothbrush when the bristles begin to look droopy or flat.

### Home Remedies

After a meal, rinse your mouth with warm salt water.

Brushing with a twig from a *kikar* or neem tree can be done once a day. However, if you have fillings in your teeth, a twig might dislodge them.

Another good thing for teeth and gums is a mango leaf. Roll a mango leaf and chew on it for some time. Discard the pulp and most of the juice. With a little of the remaining juice, massage your gums with your fingertips. It will make your gums tighten and your teeth shine. It is perfectly safe for fillings too.

*Source: Hansaben Yoga Ashram Santacruz, Mumbai*

Bits of food left between the teeth can irritate the gums and cause them to bleed. You can visit your dentist if you have bleeding gums. Eat fewer sweets and more of salads and fruits. Try home remedies to keep gums and teeth healthy.

There is an old wives' tale that for every baby you lose a tooth. This need not be true. Remember that your gums soften, not the teeth. When the body needs extra calcium to form the baby's teeth and bones and there is not enough in the mother's body, the womb will steal from the mother's bones, making them brittle. The teeth themselves are unaffected. They have to be protected by proper cleanliness.

*Leg cramps*

Leg cramps may occur suddenly in pregnancy and be quite painful. They mostly occur in the last months of pregnancy. Sluggish blood circulation, lack of calcium, and lack of Vitamin B or E are thought to cause these cramps.

Massaging the area when cramps occur is relieving. Also, point the toes inwards towards the face when the cramp occurs. Someone can hold the painful area of the leg with one hand and with the other hand guide the foot and toes to point towards the face.

A hot water bottle could be used in winter to warm your bed. Place a hot water bottle in bed before you go to sleep so that your bed is already warm.

One can increase the intake of milk products, so that the body can get the much needed calcium. Cottage cheese, milk, curds, buttermilk, cheese and greens of radish, turnip, cauliflower, *methi, dhania, pudina* and all varieties of *kerae* are good.

Whole and split *(chhilka) dals* are a good source of Vitamin B. Whole *moong*, whole *masoor*, whole *urad*, split *moong* and split *urad* are some examples of this.

Exercising to get the circulation going in the legs should also help. When you have to sit for long periods, draw the letters of the alphabet (A,B,C, etc.) with your toes, in the air. Before sleeping, walk across about a six-foot-long area, on your toes, then on your heels and lastly, on the outer sides of your feet. Done every day before sleeping at night, it has given relief to a lot of women.

Take extra salt, especially at night, in case cramps occur when you are trying to go on a salt free diet.

*Shortness of breath*

As the pregnancy advances, the uterus presses towards the lungs. This results in shortness of breath and panting when you climb even a few steps, or the need to take a deep sigh frequently. This is more so in case of a twin pregnancy, or if you are fairly short, so that the uterus feels very large. The discomfort will be more when you sit on something low, when you slump your shoulders or when you lie down. If you sit up straight, it will relieve the discomfort.

It is nothing to worry about, the discomfort will vanish with the birth of the baby.

*Palpitations*

You might feel that your heart is beating unusually fast. This is called palpitation. Sometimes you might feel your heart is missing a beat. You are more likely to notice this when you exert physically, like walking, climbing stairs, etc. It is quite normal.

It happens because your heart does a lot of extra work when you are pregnant. It needs to pump enough blood around your body to supply both you and your baby with oxygen and nutrients. Also, your blood supply increases in volume by about 40% to keep pace with the increased demands. To cope up with this extra volume of blood, the heart actually enlarges, so that it is more powerful. This enables it to pump through the extra blood without speeding up the rate of heartbeat.

Thus it is not surprising to occasionally notice a difference in the way your heart beats. However, palpitations are nothing to worry about.

*Fainting and dizziness*

Because of lowering of blood pressure, not enough oxygen reaches the brain. Sometimes this causes fainting or dizziness. Dizzy spells may also be caused by anaemia.

In the first 3 months of pregnancy, the blood pressure is lower than normal. This is why some women complain of dizziness when they first become pregnant. Some of them might actually lose consciousness for a moment or two. This is not harmful to the baby or the mother, except that the mother might injure herself if she falls to the ground in a faint.

In case you have a tendency towards dizzy spells or fainting, avoid crowded and smoky places and long journeys. Avoid moving too suddenly from a lying or sitting position.

*Itching*

Some pregnant women develop an itchy skin, and find red bumps appearing on the abdomen and breasts. This is primarily due to the stretching of the skin and can be aggravated by heavy perspiration or stress. For temporary relief try an oil massage. Women with large breasts often find that it affects them just under the breasts. Calamine lotion may have a soothing effect.

| | |
|---|---|
| *When you do not show* | Some pregnant women, who have been athletes, dancers, or who have been exercising regularly and are tall, do not show much. Their abdomen does not protrude outwards like that of other women in the same month of pregnancy. This is because they have a strong set of healthy muscles. It does not mean that something is wrong with the baby. |
| *Stretch marks* | The skin is made up of elastic and non–elastic fibres. When stretching beyond the normal limits occurs, as in pregnancy, the non-elastic fibres tend to break, causing stretch marks. At first these marks may occur as streaks. After birth they take on a kind of purple or brown shade and finally end up as whitish streaks. Excessive water retention (which does not occur as a result of drinking excess water), or weight gain can also cause stretch marks. |

These marks may appear on the stomach, breasts, bottom and thighs.

To an extent the marks may be controlled by regulating weight to avoid overstretching of the skin but the stretching on the tummy cannot be avoided as it is the result of an expanding uterus. Besides, hormonal changes that encourage water retention may cause an increase in fluid retention on your bottom and thighs, causing stretch marks to appear, even in an aware, weight-regulated woman.

The reason why stretch marks are worse in some women, is simply because the elasticity of the skin

39

varies from person to person. Women with fewer stretch marks have more elastic fibres in the skin. There is no way in which the skin's elasticity can be increased to reduce stretch marks.

Many women believe that oiling the skin helps, especially with Vitamin E oil. There is no evidence to support this theory. However, there is no harm in a gentle massage of the stretched abdomen. It is very relaxing. Moreover if you are lucky, you may find that the marks do not appear at all.

---

Your feet might swell or flatten further because of the extra weight you now carry. You might need shoes a size larger as compared to what you normally wear. Do not wear high heels, they will upset your balance, co-ordination, and posture.

  Your footwear should be flat. Avoid wearing heels during the day and walk barefoot in the evenings at home. All shoes, whether walking shoes or slippers, should have a similar height throughout pregnancy.

*Footwear*

---

Mucous membranes inside the nose and sinuses often swell up during pregnancy, on account of certain hormones that also soften up the vagina and the mouth of the womb, in preparation for birth. Some women therefore develop a permanent cold in late pregnancy. However, this will not interfere with your ability to do breathing exercises at the time of labour.

*Nasal congestion*

---

The weight of the baby is supported by the backbone, with the assistance of the muscles of the back and abdomen. When these muscles are weak, the pressure on the backbone is greater and causes discomfort. When these muscles are strong and toned up, the baby's

*Backache*

**Wrong!**

✔ **Right**

weight exerts less pressure on the backbone and no backache occurs.

Bad posture also causes backaches. A good posture is simply good balance of the different parts of the body. As you stand, gravity has the effect of constantly pulling you down to the floor, but you remain upright against the force of gravity, by using your muscles to hold yourself erect. If you allow some of your muscles to slacken, other muscles will tighten in order to compensate for the slackening resulting in bad posture and a strain on your back and other parts of your body.

Typically in pregnancy, one stands with one's bottom out and the hollow of one's back exaggerated. Instead, one should learn to stand straighter. Keep your bottom tucked in and use your abdominal muscles to support the extra weight, instead of overstretching them by just letting them go.

You will benefit by looking and feeling better, and suffering less from backache and tiredness. Also, your stomach will flatten faster after delivery. Tightening your abdominal muscles is not harmful to the baby at all. The baby is comfortably cushioned in the uterus with the amniotic fluid; it gets its supply of oxygen through the umbilical cord; and makes place for itself by nudging the intestines, bladder, liver and other organs away.

To relieve backaches, pull your tummy in, tuck your bottom in and straighten the length of your backbone against a wall.

Rest should also help soothe your backache. Do not let yourself get overtired. Lie down more often. When lying on your back with legs straight, place a small pillow or folded towel in the hollow of your back.

Or else, lie with your legs bent at the knees, feet flat on the floor. As you lie like this, flatten the hollow of your back against the floor.

If you prefer to lie on your side, place pillows as high as your hips. Bend and place the leg on the upper side, bent at the knee, on top of the pile of pillows. Place the arm on the underside, towards your back, along the length of your backbone.

Severe low backache may sometimes be caused by lack of calcium, or by the baby's position. If it is due to lack of calcium, the doctor would recommend supplementary calcium.

Upper backache may be caused by poor posture or heavy breasts. Correct your posture and wear a good well-fitting cotton bra, adjusted at the straps to carry the weight of the breasts.

Pain under the breasts or just below the ribs is common as pregnancy advances, say after the 6th month. The reason being, that, as the baby grows, it extends upwards to below the breasts and tends to push up your organs like the liver, stomach, etc., towards the chest cavity. You will find stretching your arms up, straight above your head, helps relieve discomfort, since it lifts the ribcage off the growing uterus. Also, sitting straight rather than slouching forward will be more comfortable.

*Pain under the breasts*

*Pain in the groin and sides of the abdomen*

In late pregnancy it is common to have pain in the pelvic region, since the joints of the pelvic girdle soften in preparation for birth. Avoid standing for a long time. The pain might also result from stretching of the round ligament, which holds the uterus in place.

*Tingling and numbness*

Tingling and numbness may be felt in the hands in the morning. It is caused by the pressure on the nerves and tendons by the accumulated fluid in hands and wrists. It is felt more in the morning when your wrists have accumulated fluid during the night. To relieve the discomfort, hold your hands above your head for a few minutes and point your fingers towards the ceiling and open and close your fists alternately. Try and control the swelling in your body by reducing salt in the diet.

*Swollen hands and feet*

Pregnancy can bring with it swelling of hands, feet, ankles and face. This is called oedema. Since the body retains extra water in pregnancy, a little bit of swelling is normal. Swelling can also be caused by hot weather, tight or ill-fitting shoes or exertion; but this kind of swelling generally disappears during the night, when you are comfortable and it is cooler.

Severe swelling of the hands and feet that does not go away at night could be a symptom of the onset of toxaemia and should be reported to the doctor.

Increase your protein intake and reduce salt intake. Salt encourages

### Natural Healing

According to Raikadu Balamma, a popular healer in Pastapur, Andhra Pradesh, oedema can be treated by a handful of crushed fenugreek *(methi)* leaves and about 10 grams of ginger (*adrak)* crushed separately. She mixes these to make three tablets. The woman with swelling has to swallow a tablet with water first thing each morning for 3 days. Many women have been cured by this treatment.

Source: *Touch Me, Touch-Me-Not (Women, Plants and Healing),* Published by Kali for Women, 1997

43

retention of water in the body. Avoid foods with a high concentration of salt, e.g. pickles, salted fish, cheese and *papad (see p. 67)*.

Avoid standing for long periods of time without rest. Sit whenever possible, and if possible, put your feet up on a stool.

## Behavioural Changes

Desire for abnormal foods like coal and soil is called pica. Generally it is due to lack of minerals like iron or calcium in the body. It was more common in the past. Any leaning towards pica should be dealt with by a correction of iron or vitamin deficiencies. Your doctor will tell you what your body misses and how you can correct it.

*Abnormal cravings*

It should not be confused with a desire for a particular kind of food, like chocolates, in pregnancy. That is, preference for a particular food should not be made an excuse for eating an excess of fattening and sweet things, since heavy food always leads to increased weight, which may lead to complications.

Tiredness is a sign that you need to slow down and take it easy. Try and get at least 10 hours of sleep daily. If you cannot manage it at night, sleep a few hours in the afternoon. Also try and go to bed sooner at night.

*Tiredness*

In some cases, tiredness may be caused by anaemia *(see p.58 & 64)*.

Mood swings are common in pregnancy owing to the hormonal changes associated with it. Normally stable women might find themselves going through periods of depression, with tears just beneath the surface. Or a

*Mood swings*

woman might feel high one moment and low the next moment. Warn your near and dear ones of how you feel, to avoid misunderstandings.

**Sleeplessness**

Stress and worry can cause sleeplessness. If you are worried about your pregnancy or approaching childbirth, discuss it with your spouse or doctor. It is likely that once you have voiced them, the worries will disappear.

At times although sleep comes to you when you retire to bed at night, you may be woken up in a few hours, by a desire to pass urine or by the baby kicking. Thereafter it may be difficult to go back to sleep.

Restrict your fluid intake at night or in the late evening. Try not to worry too much about not being able to go back to sleep. Recite a prayer or a poem in your mind, or, your favourite song. Avoid coffee in the evening, as it is a mild stimulant and might keep you awake at night.

A cup of hot milk just before retiring to bed will help you to relax. A warm salt water bath is also relaxing. Try and consciously relax by doing some deep breathing or the yogic *shavasana*, the corpse pose.

If you sleep in the afternoons, it would help if you stopped your afternoon nap, so that you can sleep better at night. Instead of a nap in the afternoon you could just relax for about half an hour with music or a book, putting your feet up as you do so.

**Medicines**

Avoid taking medicines on your own. Whatever medicine you take should only be under your doctor's advice, after you have informed the doctor of your pregnant condition. Indiscriminate use of certain medicines or drugs can harm the baby. It is best to keep drug intake to the minimum.

45

Travelling is no cause for worry if the pregnancy has been normal and stable. Travelling long distance is better done by train than by car or bus. Sitting for long periods should be avoided, since it causes congestion in the legs and pelvic region. In a train, movement is possible and therefore, the discomfort is reduced. Also, a pregnant woman has the need to empty her bladder frequently.

*Travelling*

Autorickshaws are safe if you are used to them. But avoid long, bumpy autorickshaw rides on rough roads. On a long, bumpy route, take a bus for most part of the journey and an autorickshaw for a small part of it. Request the driver to drive slowly.

If you have high blood pressure or if you have had a miscarriage or bleeding at the beginning of your pregnancy, then travelling by air, even in late pregnancy is not advisable, since the change in altitude may cause premature labour.

Even in a perfectly normal pregnancy, avoid travelling great distances by air in the last 6 weeks, also avoid travelling abroad, across time zones, for instance. In the last 4 weeks you must remain close to your home and hospital.

Flying in an unpressurised aircraft can cause serious oxygen deprivation to the baby in the first 3 months. However, all modern passenger aircrafts are properly pressurised.

Research has shown that smoking has a marked negative effect on the baby. Smoking after the 4th month of pregnancy causes mental and physical retardation in later childhood, i.e. retardation in the child's reading ability and in its skeletal growth.

*Smoking*

Smoking is known to reduce the size of the baby and therefore its chances of survival. Also, smokers lack Vitamin B$_{12}$, since it is used by the liver to detoxify the effects of smoking.

Smoking reduces the oxygen supply to the baby by causing constriction of the vessels in the placenta, causing intra-uterine growth retardation in the fetus. even passive smoking, that is, inhaling smoke by sitting in a smoke-filled room, or the husband smoking in the presence of the wife in the bedroom.

Smoking has also been associated with intra-uterine death, premature delivery and rupture of membranes. A doubled risk of early spontaneous abortion, stillbirth, congenital abnormality, neonatal death, pre-and post-delivery haemorrhage.

Most women who smoke find that they dislike the taste of cigarettes at the start of pregnancy. It is good for a woman to stop smoking as soon as she finds that she is pregnant. Research has shown that the first 3 months are very crucial, and women should not smoke during this time.

Smoking should be given up totally by women suffering from kidney disease, high blood pressure, pre-eclampsia and bleeding at any stage of pregnancy; also, by women who have lost a baby in the first 2 weeks of its life and who have delivered a stillborn child. Smoking would interfere with the development and function of the placenta, so that adequate nourishment and oxygen would not reach the fetus.

Cigarette smoke contains 2 harmful substances, nicotine and carbon monoxide—which do a lot of damage. Nicotine reduces blood supply to the baby, and carbon monoxide, which is like poison, enters the baby's circulation because its blood pigment has a strong affinity to it.

Alcohol in pregnancy must be avoided. In the 1960s research began to show that alcohol is teratogenic, that is, capable of causing malformations in the fetus.

*Alcohol*

Even moderate drinkers can give birth to babies with Fetal Alcohol Syndrome, that is, babies born with jitters, irritability, lethargy and weak sucking reflex.

Parents who consume alcohol can have low birth-weight babies, babies with mental retardation, and facial deformities, including flat features and cleft palates.

Even a single heavy-drinking session can impair the growth of a particular organ of the fetus, depending on the stage of development reached at that time.

Since social drinking is common, alcohol does not seem so dangerous, but remember, it is as potent as any drug or medicine taken in the form of a pill. If you are trying to conceive, or if you have just discovered that you are pregnant, cut out alcohol.

Research as to the safe limit of alcohol consumption in pregnancy is continuing. An occasional glass of wine or beer for a perfectly healthy mother may be harmless. Recent research has shown that 25% of women having as little as 2 ounces of alcohol in a week are more likely to have spontaneous abortions as compared to women who do not take alcohol at all.

Alcohol also damages the liver and uses up the $B_{12}$ vitamin in the body. It is therefore, best avoided.

Many people chew tobacco either in a *pan* (betel leaf) or plain. Tobacco leads to contractions of the blood vessels, so that blood circulation in the uterus and the placenta is impaired. Tobacco consumption during

*Tobacco chewing*

pregnancy not only diminishes birth weight and length but increases the risk of stillbirths. It is also associated with increased loss of male fetus and increased placental weight. It has also been shown that nicotine (a substance in tobacco) is excreted in breast milk, saliva and urine.

**Driving**

Driving is quite harmless if you remember to drive slowly and carefully. Avoid braking suddenly or any rash driving, since you do not want any mishap like the steering wheel pushing into your abdomen.

## Digestive Problems

**Vomiting and nausea**

With pregnancy there is decreased intestinal tone and gastric mobility. This slows down the passage of food through the digestive system and increases the possibility of the absorption of nutrients. On the other hand, it may be one of the factors leading to vomiting in early pregnancy and to constipation in later pregnancy.

Vomiting may also be caused by a rapid rise in hormones in early pregnancy. The level of the hormone gonadotrophin is reduced considerably by the 3rd or 4th month, and this is when a woman tends to feel less sick.

A woman may feel nauseous at any time of the day or night. It usually happens when the stomach is either very empty or very full. So, it makes sense to have 4 moderate meals a day, rather than a heavy lunch and a heavy dinner. Breakfast, lunch, tea and dinner can each be fairly filling, but should not give a stuffed feeling. Or else, you can

> **Home Remedies**
>
> Things that will help conquer nausea are sucking a lime or peppermint sweet, *saunf* or aniseed, strong ginger flavour, sipping iced water, herbal tea, that is, light *tulsi* or mint tea without milk, or sugar.

have 6 to 7 small meals in a day. You can make sandwiches in advance or keep biscuits, *dal* sprouts and fruits handy.

Nibbling on a biscuit or toast in the morning, before you get out of bed, helps. Also lying still for about 10 minutes before getting out of bed. Have breakfast 1 hour after waking up.

Avoid tea, coffee, fruit juice, fried and spicy food and alcohol. Eat a banana between meals.

When you find that you can keep something down, resist eating too much at once. Try eating and drinking things you would not normally eat, in order to find out what you can keep down.

Avoid strong smells. Get someone else to do the cooking. Carbohydrates generally stay down more easily. That is, bread, biscuits, rice, *chappatis*, potatoes, etc. Do not worry too much about weight gain. Discard tight clothing. Your clothes should be comfortable around the stomach and bust.

> **Home Remedies**
> A midnight snack is easier to keep down. Keep a snack by your bedside and have it in the course of the night.

Severe vomiting that continues beyond the first 3 or 4 months of pregnancy is called hyperemesis. A woman with hyperemesis is really ill, since she cannot retain any food. Some psychiatrists and obstetricians feel that it is a symptom of disturbed relationships, and if a woman can get away from anyone who is causing her stress, the vomiting will ease off.

It should be a good idea for a woman, who is vomiting at all hours of the day, to get away and live with people she knows slightly. It is a good time to visit an aunt or a relative in another town. The change will settle her down, and she will come back to cope with renewed strength.

Although vomiting does not harm the baby or the pregnancy, in some cases the doctor may recommend hospitalisation. On being admitted the woman will be fed fluids sweetened with sugar or glucose. If the woman has lost a lot of weight, and cannot keep down the fluid she is being fed, she might be put on an intravenous glucose drip. The body needs sugar for its daily requirement. In the absence of adequate intake of sugar the body starts to make acids known as ketones. When these show up in the urine, it is a sign that vomiting is severe and hospitalisation is necessary.

## Heartburn

This is common from mid-pregnancy onwards. Small amounts of food from the stomach re-enter the food pipe since the stomach valve relaxes and also because of the pressure the growing baby exerts against the stomach. If this happens several times in a day, a burning sensation is felt in the food pipe. To avoid it happening, the stomach should not be completely full or empty. In an empty stomach, acid formation causes this feeling. Sips of cold water should relieve this burning.

To sleep on a full stomach will also cause discomfort. It is a good idea to stay propped up during the night, if it gets very bad. A few extra pillows or cushions will help you stay more upright while you sleep, and it can be quite comfortable. Better still, eat dinner at 7.30 or 8 p.m.

Avoid eating spicy or vinegary foods, excessive salads and green leafy vegetables, and alcohol. Have 4 moderate meals, instead of 2 large meals, in a day.

## Flatulence

Flatulence, or wind, is not harmful, but embarrassing. Try keeping away from company when you are passing wind. Avoid gaseous foods like beans, peas, rich food, and excessive amounts of greens.

In pregnancy a muscle-relaxing hormone, called relaxin, is secreted by the body, which relaxes, among other things, the digestive system. Relaxing of the digestive system leads to its sluggishness. It therefore requires greater amounts of bulk in it, so as to aid the movement of food through the alimentary canal. Constipation is therefore common in pregnancy.

*Constipation and Piles*

If you find that you have developed a tendency towards constipation, eat less bread, rice and *maida*. Eat more *chappatis*, preferably made of unsieved flour, pulses or *dals*. Increase the intake of fruits, salads and vegetables.

*Bhindi* or lady's fingers can be eaten. Dried figs *(anjir)* are also very good, and easily available at dry–fruit shops. An increase in fluid intake helps, so drink more water. Drink 2 glasses of water on waking up in the morning.

Isab Gol (fleaseed husks) can be taken regularly. It is available in packets at chemists' shops. Follow the instructions on the packet. Avoid allopathic laxative pills.

If constipation lingers over a period and is not treated, it can cause veins around the anus to protrude, from straining that accompanies constipation, leading to piles or permanently protruding veins around the anus.

If piles occur, keep constipation in check and avoid spicy food.

This sometimes occurs in pregnancy and it

*Diarrhoea*

should be reported to the doctor if it persists for more than a day or two. Iron tablets can cause it in some women. In such cases it can be remedied by simply changing the brand of the tablets.

> **Home Remedies**
> In case of diarrhoea having a mixture of black tea and a slightly over ripe mashed banana helps. One could put the mashed banana in a soup bowl and pour black tea over it. Cool it before having it.

Many women who add lots of fruits and vegetables to their diet find that their stool is a little loose or that they pass stool twice in a day. This should not be confused with diarrhoea.

## Urinary Tract Infection

*Frequent urination*

In pregnancy one urinates more often as the growing uterus puts pressure on the bladder and restricts the space normally reserved for the storage of urine. The problem will stay until the birth of the baby. At the most you can limit the intake of fluids in the evening, so that you do not have to wake up at night too often to go to the toilet.

*Urinary tract infection*

An infection in the urinary tract causes inflammation of the bladder and urethra, the pipe through which urine is passed. This is called cystitis. Cystitis is a common complaint that could occur in pregnancy.

The first symptom is usually the desire to pass urine more frequently, sometimes only minutes after having already done so. Most of the time you will not be able to pass much urine, perhaps only a trickle or not at all. This can be accompanied by a burning sensation or stinging. When you do manage to pass some urine, it may be very dark yellow in colour, and in extreme cases, streaked with blood.

This infection is easily caused in women because of

the female anatomy; since the openings of the urethra, vagina and anus are all very close together. Germs from the stool get transmitted very easily to the urethra and vagina.

It is important to consult your doctor as soon as possible if you have an attack of cystitis, because if it is left untreated the infection can travel to the kidney and be very painful and dangerous. Cystitis is very easily treated, once diagnosed early. A course of antibiotics will soon rid the infection.

*Cystitis*

To relieve the symptoms of cystitis immediately, drink a glass of water every half hour, to dilute the strength of the urine, and to help flush the infection through, before it gets a chance to take a hold. Any watery liquid will do, for example, a lemon or barley drink, weak tea, *lassi*, etc. This helps make the urine less acidic (alkaline urine is inhospitable to germs) and therefore less painful when passed or excreted.

If you have suffered from cystitis several times before, and think you may be prone to developing the infection again, there are 2 things you can do to lessen the likelihood of an attack. First, drink plenty of fluids. It is a good idea to make it a habit to drink 2 glasses of water on waking up in the morning. It will also help relieve constipation. Second, be more hygienic. Every time you pass stool, wash the anal area not only with water, but with soap and water; and do not bring your hand forward towards your urethra as you do so. Better still, wash from behind. During your bath, use soap and water to wash the vaginal area. Similarly wash your anus thoroughly.

It is normal to have increased vaginal discharge in pregnancy, because the glands at the mouth of the womb

*Vaginal discharge*

54

increase their output.

The discharge is actually cleansing the vagina and keeping it free of infection, as well as lubricating the tissues of the vagina as they become thicker, softer, and more elastic in preparation for birth. During subsequent pregnancies the discharge will be less. Make sure you wear cotton underwear to allow your skin to breathe.

If you notice a change in the discharge from white to yellow or green, and if it causes itching or irritation, becomes thicker or smells unpleasant, you probably have an infection. It is a minor, harmless infection called thrush, candida or monilia.

It is easily treated with creams or pessaries, under the doctor's guidance. Sometimes the pessaries may be supplemented with antibiotics. Early treatment is desirable to prevent future complications.

During the advanced stage of pregnancy, that is, if your baby is due within a month and you have a discharge that looks like the beginning of a period, a thick mucus discharge, tinted with dried blood (pink or brown), it is a sign that your body is getting ready for birth. Take it as a signal. It is just that, and not an emergency.

## Conditions Needing Special Attention

*Vaginal bleeding*   In early pregnancy, vaginal bleeding may be caused because the level of your pregnancy hormone is not sufficiently high to stop your period. The bleeding will be scanty and it will occur when a period would have been due. Such bleeding is not a miscarriage. The doctor may give an injection of progesterone hormone or advise bed rest.

Sometimes a few drops of blood may appear after intercourse, or a vaginal examination by the doctor.

Late in pregnancy, bright-red bleeding, like that which flows at the height of a period, is serious, although quite rare. It can be caused by the placenta, the organ that nourishes the baby, detaching from the wall of the uterus. The seriousness will depend on how large a portion of the placenta has separated from the uterus. The doctor should be informed immediately.

You might be advised to go to the hospital for bed rest. Lying down increases the blood flow to the uterus and if the placenta is not firmly rooted, gives it a chance to root itself firmly to the wall of the uterus. If bleeding stops and all is well with the baby, you will be permitted to go home in a few days. In this case it is wise to avoid intercourse and orgasm until after the baby is born.

Sometimes bleeding is caused by the placenta lying too low between the baby's head and the mouth of the womb. This is called placenta previa and means delivery by Caesarean section. It could also mean bed rest, at home or hospital, before the birth of the baby.

Any physical movement such as running or jumping can temporarily raise the blood pressure, but it returns to normalcy after a period of rest.

Excessive weight gain could raise blood pressure. Also, a stressful lifestyle, or a nervous, easily agitated and highly strung person, tends to be prone to blood pressure.

It is therefore important to rest when you feel you are getting tired and tense. Avoid unnecessary nerve-racking activity, like watching a late night horror/violent movie.

Rising blood pressure will be a cause for concern to your doctor. At every visit to your doctor, the blood pressure is measured, the reason being that rising blood pressure could herald the beginning of certain complications of pregnancy, such as toxaemia, which need special attention and care.

If the diastolic blood pressure (the lower figure of the recorded level, e.g. 120/70) rises by as much as 20, you are considered to have high blood pressure or hypertension. Bed rest will be prescribed, since the placenta will work more efficiently if you stay in bed. In late pregnancy, many obstetricians induce labour if the diastolic reading of your blood pressure rises up to 90 or above.

If you have high blood pressure, try taking a warm bath before going to bed at night. It will help you relax and sleep better.

## Toxaemia and Pre-Eclampsia

*Toxaemia:*
*When rings*
*do not fit*

Toxaemia usually occurs only during the last few weeks of pregnancy and is recognised by 3 typical symptoms. Any of these symptoms appearing by itself does not mean you have toxaemia. It is only when they appear together that they spell toxaemia. The first symptom is increased blood pressure. The second sign is swelling of hands, feet and face, the third sign is the appearance of protein in the urine.

These are warning signals. If they are not heeded, convulsions may occur. The toxaemia has then become a serious condition known as eclampsia.

57

Vigilant pre-natal health care can prevent this condition or make it less serious. Once a woman is excreting a high proportion of protein in her urine, pregnancy is not likely to continue for longer than 2 weeks.

A well-balanced diet, with more protein and less carbohydrates and salt, reduces the incidence of toxaemia. Rest will also help.

If symptoms continue, the woman is usually put into a hospital for further treatment, and if necessary, early delivery of the baby. However, once the conditions are identified, complete bed rest in hospital with careful monitoring of the symptoms is usually enough to prevent it from getting worse.

Toxaemia can harm the unborn baby. If it progresses unchecked, it can cause the placenta to fail, and lead to premature labour before the baby is mature enough to survive. When toxaemia becomes eclampsia, it can cause fits and coma. The following are signs of eclampsia: headache, flashing lights, nausea, vomiting and pain in the abdomen.

Toxaemia and eclampsia should not be taken lightly. Starting as a minor ailment they can develop into a dangerous disease.

---

In pregnancy, blood tests are taken to find out the haemoglobin content. Haemoglobin is present in the red blood cells, and is the means by which oxygen is conveyed from the lungs to the cells in the body, including the baby in the womb. If there is not enough haemoglobin in the mother's blood, there may not be enough oxygen reaching the baby for its optimum growth and development.

*Anaemia*

Haemoglobin levels tend to drop in pregnancy,

**Home Remedies**

To increase haemoglobin levels, soak one raisin *(kishmish)* overnight in water. In the morning boil it in a cup of milk, then drink the milk and eat the raisin.

On day two soak 2 raisins overnight in water. In the morning boil them in a cup of milk, then drink the milk and eat the raisins.

Likewise go on to 3, 4, 5, 6, 7, 8 and finally 9 raisins. Then go back to 8, 7, 6, 5, 4, 3, 2, and finally one raisin.

On completion of 18 days your haemoglobin level is likely to rise.

*Source: Anand P. Verma,*
*Accupressurist*

since the fluid volume of the mother's blood increases, so that more fluid-carrying nutrients become available to the baby. However, if the haemoglobin falls below 9gms/100ml, a woman is considered anaemic.

A woman who is anaemic feels tired, exhausted, irritable, lethargic, weak and over worked, even though she may be doing little physical work. She might also experience shortness of breath and dizzy spells.

If a woman is found to be anaemic, she should increase her daily intake of iron, until the required haemoglobin level is reached. This can be done by taking a course of iron tablets, and by adding iron-rich foods in the diet.

Foods rich in iron are green cabbage leaves, cauliflower leaves, mustard leaves or *sarson*, leafy greens, *ganth gobhi* or knol khol greens, mint or *pudina, dhania* or coriander leaves, jaggery, eggs, etc. Although spinach has iron, most of it cannot be used by the body, because other substances present in spinach block absorption of iron by the blood.

If a woman avoids putting on too much weight in pregnancy, she will need less haemoglobin to sustain her body. Unnecessary weight gain requires extra blood, haemoglobin, oxygen and nutrients, thus overworking all the mechanisms of the body. Hence, excessive weight gain always works to your disadvantage.

*Rhesus–negative*  All blood is either rhesus-negative or rhesus-positive.

You run a risk only if you have a rhesus-negative blood group while your husband has a rhesus-positive blood group. A routine blood test at the beginning of the pregnancy will show whether you are rhesus-positive or negative. There is no symptom of rhesus incompatibility that you will notice.

If you are a rhesus-negative mother bearing a rhesus-positive baby, some of the baby's red cells may leak into your blood circulation. This is most likely in late pregnancy or at the time of delivery. Your body responds to the baby's blood as it would to an invader and your natural defence mechanisms will produce antibodies against it. If these antibodies leak back to the baby's circulation, they can destroy a large number of the baby's blood cells and cause severe anaemia and jaundice in the newborn.

In the first baby there is not enough time for this to happen, since the leak mostly occurs at the time of delivery. But the mother's antibodies can damage the blood cells of any rhesus-positive baby carried by the mother in future. The antibodies can vigorously attack the baby's blood so that the baby might get anaemia, jaundice or brain damage and may not survive.

In order to avoid this happening, an injection of anti-D immunoglobulin can be given to a rhesus-negative mother in pregnancy or immediately after the birth of a rhesus-positive baby. This injection is a serum which is to be given within 48 hours after the birth of a baby. It stops the mother's biological defence mechanism from acting against the foreign rhesus substances. A fresh injection is given after every delivery, miscarriage or abortion. It is possible for blood from an aborted fetus to enter the mother's bloodstream.

| | |
|---|---|
| *German Measles, Rubella* | This is a mild but very infectious disease that lasts a few days. It is caused by a virus and may cause a slight rash and fever, sometimes accompanied by swollen glands and aching joints. On the other hand, it may go unnoticed. The rash is the main sign, and lasts only 12 to 24 hours. If you fail to see a doctor when the rash occurs, a blood test taken 2 weeks later will show a high-level of antibodies from recent infection and confirm the diagnosis. |

Rubella has grave consequences for the unborn child. If you suffer from it in the first 3 months of pregnancy it may cause deafness, blindness, and congenital heart disease or any other type of abnormality. Later in pregnancy the risk is much less, and could be restricted to deafness. The virus may also cause a miscarriage, low birth-weight baby or stillbirth. If you catch rubella in the first 3 months of pregnancy, your doctor will advise a medical termination of pregnancy.

If you have been in contact with someone who has measles or has recently had measles, or who develops measles within 2 or 3 days of seeing you, consult your doctor. A couple of blood tests done 2 weeks apart will help the doctor decide whether the pregnancy should be continued or terminated.

Do not be shy to avoid relatives or friends when they have measles in the house. Tell them it is doctor's orders. Absent yourself from your place of work if there is measles there.

Mothers should immunise their daughters against rubella when they are around 10 to 14 years of age.

If you are not sure whether you have had rubella, a blood test for rubella antibodies will make it clear. If a blood test shows that you have never had rubella, you can be immunised after your baby is born, to avoid worry in future. However, the inoculation should not be taken in pregnancy, and once taken in the non-pregnant state, conception should be avoided for next 3 months.

# 5. Diet in Pregnancy and After

## Eating for Two

There is a common belief that a pregnant woman should eat for 2 people. This is not necessary, but it is essential to eat the right food. One needs to eat nutritious food. Everything that you eat should have good food value, that is, one should eat for 2 but not twice as much.

> We may live without books –
> what is knowledge but grieving?
> We may live without hope –
> what is hope but deceiving?
> We may live without passion –
> what is passion but pining?
> But where is the man that
> can live without dining?
>
> Owen Meredith

## A Parasite

The baby within is like a parasite; that is, it takes the nutrients it requires, regardless of whether you have enough or not. It takes, for instance, enough iron to store in its liver for the first 3 months of its life, not to mention the iron it uses up for the formation of its blood.

Then it takes calcium from your body to form its bones and the foundation of its teeth. If you do not consume enough calcium, it is going to take calcium away from your bones. You cannot afford to let this happen, for you will need good health and strength to look after your baby after it is born. So you must make it a point to eat well.

## Foods You Need

The foods you need to take are those rich in iron, calcium and proteins.

*Iron*
Iron is present in green leafy vegetables. It is a good idea to keep *pudina* or *dhania* (mint or coriander) chutney handy. Make small quantities of it and store in a covered bottle in the refrigerator. Prepare it every 3rd or 4th day. Two teaspoons of chutney a day will meet a good part of your daily iron requirement. You can use it instead of butter to spread on bread when making a sandwich *(see p.58).* Iron is also present in *kishmish* or raisins. It is present in *gur* or jaggery and powdered brown sugar, which is different from caramelised white sugar. It is present in any dish cooked in an iron pan. However, food cooked in an iron pan gets black, unless the pan is treated with a thin layer of oil, and heated before being used for cooking.

Dried fish is especially rich in both iron and calcium. So are yeast tablets, radish leaves, knol-khol or *ganth gobhi* leaves, *kerae* or leafy greens, cauliflower leaves, etc.

The iron in spinach is not easily absorbed. Vitamin C promotes iron absorption.

Soyabean, *kabuli channa* or whole bengal gram, *kala channa* or horse gram, *rajma* or kidney beans, *sabut moong* or green gram are also rich in both iron and calcium.

Also, if you do not sieve the *atta* or flour before making *chapattis* you will get iron and Vitamin B from it. Clean, wash and dry wheat for this purpose, before sending it to the flour mill. If you lack the time, buy the cleaner, more expensive wheat.

*Calcium*
Calcium is available from milk and milk products. You must drink about 3 glasses of milk in a day. You can have milk in whichever form you like. As curd,

cheese, *paneer*, custard, buttermilk or *lassi*, even curry made from curds.

Calcium is also present in green leafy vegetables. But if you have gas or flatulence, heartburn or sour burps, you should not have too much of green leafy vegetables. About one tablespoon at a time is enough.

Eggs and lemons are a good source of calcium. Lack of calcium in the long run makes you weak. It can also cause severe backache or cramps. It causes irritability, for its lack causes the nerves to twitch. It is a good idea to take a cup of hot milk before you sleep.

---

*Protein*

Protein is the body's building material. You need protein not only to build a baby's body but also to look after the wear and tear and maintenance of your own body.

If you have an egg a day, and pulses or *dals* with your meals, you should get enough proteins.

However, if you are a pure vegetarian and do not eat eggs at all, you must take care to see that your diet contains adequate protein. *Dals* are a good source of protein, but not the best.

The best source is a mixture of *dal* and wheat. A combination of *dal* and wheat is complementary, since together pulses and wheat provide a mixture of all essential amino acids or proteins. A mixture of *dal* and rice is also a good source of protein.

For non-vegetarians who eat meat at least thrice a week, the protein intake is adequate. But if you eat meat only when you eat out or entertaining at parties, you should consider yourself to be a vegetarian.

Another good source of protein is milk and milk products, that is, *paneer*, curd and so on. Nuts like peanuts or *moong phali*, almonds or *badams*, cashewnuts or *kajus*, etc., are also a good source of protein. *Badam* traditionally is considered superior to other nuts, but nutritionally it is of no superior value. Nuts also have a fair amount of fat.

*Channa* too is a very good source of protein, be it *channa dal*, *besan*, or the roasted *channa* sold by *channawalas*. *Channa* is a good thing to keep handy to eat between meals. You can eat it instead of biscuits or fried *namkeens*. It will be better for your figure as well as for your nutrition. You can keep *channas* mixed with little pieces of jaggery in a jar to eat when hungry. While *channa* will provide you with protein, jaggery will provide you with iron.

Another good source of protein is soyabean and soyabean products. You can get soyabean products in the market. All you have to do is soak the soya nuggets or granules in warm salt water. Prepare your favourite *masala*, it could be onion, capsicum, tomato. Then squeeze the nuggets or granules thoroughly and add them to the masala, when it is done. It makes a nutritious dish. You could also add the nuggets or granules to whichever vegetable is made, to increase its quantity and nutrition.

Or else you could buy soyabean in 1 kilogram packets, soak them overnight like kidney beans or *rajma*, and cook them in a similar way, in a gravy, the next morning.

Further you could buy about 5 kilograms of soyabean, have it ground into flour or *atta* at the flour mill or *chakki*, and store it separately at home. When you knead your flour for *chapattis*, add a handful of the soyabean flour to it. There will be no difference in taste, and the whole family will get more nutrition.

# Wholesome Foods

A cereal, pulse and vegetable mixture makes a very wholesome meal. For example, *dosa or idli* with *sambhar* and coconut chutney.

Another such combination can be made with *parathas*. If you make a dough of half *besan* or chick-pea flour and half wheat flour and add to it chopped radish or *mooli* leaves or green cabbage leaves, it will make quite a wholesome meal. Also, a *paratha* made of a mixed flour of wheat, horse gram or *kala channa* and barley or *jawar* with radish or cabbage leaves chopped in it is good. These *parathas* are a meal in themselves and can be eaten with curd for breakfast, lunch, or dinner.

Pickles have a high concentration of salt and are to be avoided if you are getting swollen hands and feet. Butter should be avoided if you are overweight.

Another nutritious food is sprouted whole green gram or *moong dal*. It is best eaten raw. Cooking reduces its food value. It has protein and Vitamins B and C. Clean, wash

Food groups at the bottom of the pyramid nourish your body well.

Food groups on the top of the pyramid damage your body when taken in excess.

salt, sugar, jams, preservatives, pickles, cold drinks, cheese, ready to eat packed foods ajino-moto (MSG)

Butter, cream, pastries, chocolates, ice creams, *pakoras, jalebis, mathis*

*Chappatis*, bread, rice porridge *(dalia)*

pulses, *dals*, lentils *(rajma, channa, lobia)*, milk, curd, eggs, meat and other non-vegetarian products, *idli, sambhar, paneer*, soyabean, *khichri* with curd oats

lemons, fresh seasonal fruits and vegetables, dry fruits, raw nuts, fruit or vegetable juice, green *chutney*, tender coconut water

*Sprout Farms*

A 'sprout farm' of acrylic trays is available in the market. You place soaked lentils in the trays and pour a glass of water on the first tray. It drains to the trays below and sprouting occurs.

and soak the *dal* at least 4–5 hours in summer and 8–10 hours in winter. You could soak it overnight. Then drain the water and place in a large jar. Tie a cloth over the mouth of the jar. Pour water and drain out, not leaving any water in the jar. Repeat twice more during the day. In a day or two it should sprout. It can be added to chopped salad, to cucumber cubes or grated radish. It can be sprinkled on vegetables or added to sandwich fillings. It can be made into a savoury by itself, by adding lemon juice, chopped onions, coriander, green chillies and salt. You can sprout any dried beans or pulses in a similar fashion, for example, horse gram or *kala channa*, Egyptian lentil or *sabut kala masoor dal*, etc.

Potato is a highly misunderstood vegetable. Although potatoes do have carbohydrates, they are 99.9% fat-free and 100% cholesterol-free. They have vitamins B and C, and some proteins. Boiled potatoes are a good and cheap source of nutrition. Potatoes become fattening only when they are fried. At tea time one can have boiled potatoes with salt, chopped onions, lemon juice and chopped mint or coriander leaves added to them. Potatoes contain more moisture or water than cereals; therefore they contain fewer calories as compared to cereals.

If you keep boiled potatoes in the fridge, they can be handy when you need a quick bite, but lack the time to cook. Do not skin or cut potatoes before you boil them; that way they lose nutrition. Boil them in their jacket. When boiled, the skin should not break.

Then there is the highly recommended category of seasonal fruits and vegetables. Guavas, oranges, watermelons, and bananas. Cabbages and carrots eaten raw will give you vitamins and minerals.

## Tea, Coffee and Cola Drinks and Chocolates

Excessive amounts of tea, coffee and cola drinks and chocolates should be avoided. They contain caffeine and other related substances like tannic acid, which impair and upset digestion.

Caffeine is a diuretic, that is, it causes more urine to be passed. This also washes away essential salts and water soluble vitamins. Further, it reduces absorption of iron and calcium. It can also cause sleep disturbances, anxiety and heartburn.

The amount of caffeine present in a cup of tea or coffee depends on the quality used and the amount of time taken to brew it. The more bitter it is, the more the caffeine content.

## To Avoid Putting On Too Much Weight

You must make sure you do not eat out of compulsion when you get tense. Instead, have a warm water bath with a spoonful of salt added to it. It is very relaxing. Or, start some activity like tidying your cupboard, baking a cake, embroidery, making pickles, etc.

Avoid white sugar as far as possible. Palm sugar and sugar made from powdered jaggery have nutritional elements in them; but white sugar is so overprocessed that 99% of its non-carbohydrate constituents are taken away from it, and it ends up as a plain energy–giving carbohydrate.

> *Methods of Cooking*
>
> Steaming is the best method of cooking as loss of nutrients is minimal. Boiling is good only if the water in which food has been boiled is also consumed. Frying, overcooking, and reheating cause a loss of nutrients and are best avoided.

Sugar is quickly digested, and is readily absorbed by the body, giving a tremendous lift of energy. This lift lasts until the sugar gets used up, and immediately one feels like eating something sweet again, to get over the low feeling that follows. So you develop a sweet tooth. What you do is that you inhibit the body's ability to produce the necessary energy from all other food. The body takes energy from sugar instead and the other energy is converted into fat. This would also apply to women who have several cups of sweet tea or several glasses of cold drinks a day.

If you feel you are developing a sweet tooth, the first thing to do is to have naturally sweet things instead. Example: Jaggery, raisins, mango, *chikoo*, honey, dates, etc. These sweet things will also give you nutrition, along with sweetness. Avoid chocolates, sweets, lollipops, ice creams, cakes, pastries, etc. Then switch to substituting a few sweet things with cheese, *channa*, apple, carrot, cucumber, sprouted *moong dal*, etc.

Gradually wean yourself away from your addiction for sweet things. Make it a slow but sure process. Be gentle, but firm, with yourself and you will find that you have retrained your taste buds by the end of it, and your desire for sweets will have diminished.

Do not use sweetex or other sugar substitutes. Remember, you are trying to cultivate a new taste. It is hard to stop craving for sugar if you take artificial sweeteners.

Avoid excessive oil in your cooking. Reduce the number of deep fried things you eat. For example, chips and *pakoras*, *puris*, fried *namkeens*, fried *papads* etc. When you have made a vegetable, there should be no oil left in the serving dish after the vegetable has been eaten. If oil remains, it is a sign that the oil used was in excess. Also, when you make curries, there should be no oil floating on the surface of the curry.

Kidney beans or *rajma*, chick peas or *kabuli channa*, horse gram or *kala channa*, all kind of pulses or *dals* can be boiled with salt, turmeric, *garam masala*, onion, ginger and a teaspoon of oil; and eaten with vegetables and *chapattis*. Avoid fried *masalas* in them. Thick rich *masala* curries are fattening. So are white sauce, thick soup, mayonnaise and foods laced with creamy sauces. All highly refined foods should be avoided, because most of the goodness or nutrition has been taken away from them. *Maida* and sugar-based foods would come under this category; also *samosas*, cakes, noodles, white bread, *jalebis*, jams, rice, *kachoris*, *mathris*, etc.

Interestingly, *khoya*, besan and *paneer*-based Indian sweets also give protein, apart from being loaded with sugar. Bengali *mithai*, *ladoos*, *rasgullas*, *channa murkhii*, *barfi*, *patisas*, are some examples.

If you tend to eat a lot at meals, fill yourself with *lassi*, raw vegetables or fruit. Do not add *ghee* to your *dal* or *chappatis*.

## Body Weight

How much weight should a woman put on in pregnancy is a matter of great interest and controversy. Earlier the permitted weight was 9 to 10 kg. Then it became 12.5 kg and now it is accepted that it may be a little higher than 12.5 kg.

If at the start of pregnancy you were underweight, you can take the

| *Estimate of Expected Weight Increase in Pregnancy* | |
|---|---|
| Fetus and placenta | 5.0 kg |
| Water | 1-1.5 kg |
| Uterus | 0.5-1 kg |
| Breasts | 1-1.5 kg |
| Fat storage in tissues | 4-4.5 kg |
| Total expected weight gain | 13.5 kg |

*Source:* Obstetrics Illustrated, *Churchill Livingston, 1980*

71

advantage of putting on more weight than a woman who started pregnancy being overweight. If you have a tendency to gain weight more rapidly than other women, you will have to be careful with the weight increase.

One thing is for sure, pregnancy is not a time to diet or try and remain slim. If you do so, you will be harming the baby.

All the weight you put on is not added to you, it is needed by your body to support and nourish the baby. After birth, a lot of fat laid down in the tissues is used up to breastfeed the baby. Women who do not feed their babies find it difficult to lose the weight they put on in their tissues; that is, on their hips, back, thighs, etc.

> **Percentage Weight Increase During Pregnancy**
>
> On an average a woman puts on a total of 25% of her non-pregnant weight.

In the first 3 months of pregnancy there may not be any weight gain. Weight might actually fall as a result of nausea, vomiting and loss of appetite. Gain in weight usually starts in the 3rd month. Weight gain up to the 5th month is not usually very great. It could account for 25% of the total weight increase. The greatest increase occurs in the 5th, 6th and 7th months. However, it should not exceed 1 kilogram in any 1 week. Excessive weight gain at this time is associated with toxaemia and the doctor may ask you to watch your weight if she finds the weight gain excessive. After 7½ months the rate of weight increase slows down until the 9th month after which there is very often no weight gain in the last 4 weeks of pregnancy.

According to Dr. Tom Brewer, an American obstetrician, nutrition is important. His theories are based on a series of controlled antenatal experiments, and go against the widely held belief that the baby is a

72

parasite, and takes whatever it needs, regardless of the mother's nutrition. He believes that even mild degrees of under-nutrition in the mother especially in the last few weeks of pregnancy, can interfere with the normal growth and development of the baby's brain. He and his wife discuss this in their book, *What Every Pregnant Woman Should Know*, New York, 1979. Many doctors now feel

| *Estimated Rate of Weight Increase* | |
|---|---|
| 1 to 3 months | No weight gain |
| 3 to 5 months | 25% of weight increase |
| 5 to 7½ months | 50% of weight increase |
| 7½ to 9 months | 25% of weight increase |
| 9th month | No weight gain. |

that even 16 kg (35 pounds, and up is a reasonable weight gain for some women. In case of twins, 18 kg and above (40 to 50 pounds) weight gain may not be excessive.

When a mother is undernourished, her uterus and placenta do not grow enough. The baby will weigh less than the normal birth weight of over 5½ pounds. During delivery, contractions may be poor. Delivery may have to be induced and Caesarean section is often necessary.

## Diet in Labour

There is a widely held belief that if you have a glass of milk with *ghee*, or have almond or *badam* milk before going to the hospital, it helps. However, once labour is established (i.e. when one contraction lasts a whole minute), your digestion slows down greatly and the body concentrates on the birth.

At this stage of established labour, if you have eaten something heavy, it will remain in the stomach and make you feel like vomiting. On the other hand, light things eaten in labour will get digested and will have passed through the stomach, giving your body energy.

Therefore if you have started labour and are hungry, eat something light, like glucose biscuits, sago, beaten rice, toast with jam. In other words, eat carbohydrates and avoid fat and protein.

Above all, learn to listen to your body; if you feel like eating, eat something light. If you do not feel like eating, don't. You can have sips of water with sugar, glucose or honey mixed in it, if you feel you need some energy. These things do not need time to get digested and get absorbed immediately by the body, giving you instant energy. *Mishri*, toffees, sweets, lollipops can also be had. Tea, coffee or *nimbupani* should be avoided as they cause a lot of acidity which can be a problem, if anaesthesia has to be administered.

If your labour is well established, you will simply not have the desire to eat, even if your favourite dish is placed before you.

## Diet when Breastfeeding

Remember, when you are pregnant or when feeding the baby, you need a lot of nutrition; so it is a wrong time to diet. A woman who is feeding the baby needs more calories than a woman who is pregnant. In pregnancy, a woman needs 300 more calories than she normally would, whereas a woman feeding a baby would need 550 more calories.

Most women who feed their babies do feel ravenously hungry; a fact that shows you the importance of listening to your body and having faith in it. If you feel hungry, you must eat. A newborn baby needs about 120 calories per kilo per day, and weighs about 3 kilograms. Therefore the baby should get about 360 calories from milk. The mother uses more than 400 calories to nourish the baby.

In fact, a lot of weight that you put on during pregnancy consists of fat deposits, placed by nature, to be used up while feeding. If you continue to eat wisely, you can lose weight while feeding.

A woman feeding a baby should avoid too many spices, since these could give a peculiar smell to the milk, making it repulsive to the baby. She should drink plenty of fluids in any form, be it milk, soup, *nimbupani* or *lassi*, to make up for the loss of her body fluid in making breast milk. She does not need to drink lots of milk to make milk. In a relaxed mother the milk flows more easily. Less water does not reduce the amount of milk produced, but it makes mother's urine very concentrated which is unhealthy for her.

A woman feeding a baby can have a normal non-spicy diet, with greater concentration on pulses, green vegetables and milk.

Alcohol and cigarettes are to be avoided. But a glass of beer or wine is permissible as both have a very low alcohol content, which relaxes the mother. Beer being barley based increases milk supply.

## Our Traditional Recipes

A word about our traditional recipes of *ladoos, panjiri,* dry fruit or *mewa*, jaggery, or whatever else you may make, to feed a woman who has just delivered a baby. They contain ingredients that are traditionally believed to be beneficial to a woman who has just delivered a baby.

The point is to have the traditional recipes in moderation. Eat about 3 to 4 tablespoons of *panjiri,*

## To Get the Maximum Goodness from Your Food

■ Clear vegetable soup is very nutritious. All the vitamins, minerals, proteins, etc. from the vegetables are passed into the soup. Thick soups are not good, as flour and fat are used to thicken them.

■ Greens, like *kerae, palak, methi, sarson, bathua, cholai,* should be washed first and then chopped. If you cut them first and then wash them, you will lose most of the water–soluble vitamins while washing.

■ Keep your vegetables away from heat and light. Heat and bright sunlight destroy some of the vitamins. Further destruction comes with cooking, so that by the time you eat it, a fair amount of vitamins are lost. Boil potatoes whole.

■ With fruits and vegetables avoid peeling if possible, or peel lightly, e.g. carrots, apples, pears. Wash vegetables and fruits before peeling, not afterward.

■ Do not overcook vegetables; keep them crunchy. Try and cook just before eating, in order to avoid reheating. Avoid storing cooked vegetables in the fridge for more than 24 hours. When you reheat food, first leave it outside the fridge for about ½ an hour so that the change of temperature is not too sudden. Avoid over cooking vegetables to death. Steaming in the pressure cooker protects vitamins.

■ It is best to use stainless steel utensils for cooking, since it is a metal that does not react to the food, like many other metals do. If you do not have them, the next best thing is to transfer food into stainless steel or plain glass bowls as soon as it is cooked.

or ½ or 1 *ladoo* with your early morning tea, when you know that activity will follow; or after a period of activity. Do not eat it as dessert after dinner and go to sleep. That is the best way to put on weight.

Overeating of anything heavy like ice cream, chocolates, *mithai* or pastries can make you put on weight, so why blame *panjiri*?

An interesting example illustrating the wisdom of our traditional practices comes to mind. In parts of South India, a woman who has delivered a baby is given water to drink in which an iron rod has been boiled. This makes it a wonderful iron rich drink. On account of monthly periods and childbearing, women generally lack iron and therefore are often prescribed iron tablets. Boiled water would also be safer to drink, since boiling destroys germs or infection present in it.

## Ghee

If you take *ghee* regularly, but do not do much work in the house and do not go for regular walks either, it could result in extra weight and stiff joints, making delivery difficult. However, if you are active and if you are not overweight, and if you do not have any cholesterol problem, you can go ahead and have *ghee*.

Over the years several women have said that eating butter or *badam rogan* or *ghee* in the last month of pregnancy helped them to have an easy delivery. This needs to be medically validated.

As such fats in the diet help in the absorption of fat soluble vitamins A,D,E and K.

All these factors could be of significance in relation to childbirth. For instance, keeping infection away would be useful, strong bones and good skin, and blood that clots could all be of enormous help.

---

### A Recipe

YOU WILL NEED:

| | |
|---|---|
| *ghee* (clarified butter) | 1 tbsp |
| *sooji* (cream of wheat) | 1 tbsp |
| *chotti elaichi* (small green cardamom) | 1 |
| *badam* (almonds) | 2 to 3 |
| milk | 1 glass |
| sugar | to taste |

METHOD

Warm *ghee*, add *sooji* to it and cook till light brown. Add milk and bring to a boil. Cook on a slow fire for 5 minutes so that the *ghee* blends with the milk. Add sugar, crushed *elaichi* and *badam*. Drink while hot the first thing in the morning starting from the 9th month and continuing till the birth.

Source: Sonia Bajaj

---

| Fat Soluble Vitamins | |
|---|---|
| Vitamin | Benefits |
| A | Prevents infection |
| D | Makes bones strong |
| E | Makes skin healthy |
| K | Helps in blood clotting |

1 gram of *ghee* has 9 calories. 1 tablespoon of ghee has 15 grams of ghee and therefore 135 calories. According to *Dietary Guidelines for Indians* published by the National Institution of Nutrition, Hyderabad, 1998, 'Visible fat intake should be increased during pregnancy and lactation to 30 grams and 45 grams respectively.'

15 grams of fat therefore falls within permissible limits. However, for today's aware, weight-conscious women, who do not want to put on too much weight, here are a couple of tips. When you add one tablespoon of *ghee* or butter to your diet in the 9th month, you can avoid other intake of calories like puddings, chocolates, cold drinks, foods with thick gravies, fried foods etc. Or else you can increase your calorie expenditure by going for long walks, which will also be beneficial in preparing your body for an easy and natural childbirth.

One could have a tablespoon of pure home made butter or a tablespoon of pure home made *ghee* in the last month of pregnancy. Butter could be consumed with *chapatti, paratha* or *dal*. The *ghee* could be had in a cup of hot milk, sweetened as preferred.

# Tips on Weight Control

■ Learn to relax before a party. When you are relaxed you will not have an urge to reach out for snacks. When you are jittery, you will tend to eat more. Lack of sleep and rest, the caffeine in coffee and colas can make you jittery. Apart from the jitters, anxiety makes you overeat. When you are anxious about some problem, you tend to find comfort in food. It is therefore important to eat at regular hours and not munch between meals. If you reach out for food every time you feel anxious, you will aggravate your weight problem and looking at your overweight self will lead you to further despair. It will give you a poor self-image and lack of confidence. You will tend to console yourself further with food.

■ If this applies to you, you should learn to take responsibility for your body and its needs. You should be in control of your food and not let your food control you. This does not mean that you should starve yourself for long periods

and then overeat. If you do starve yourself, you are most likely to overeat, because when no food has been eaten, the blood sugar level drops and you crave for food. Therefore it will not be surprising if you lose control. Never skip a meal. Regular eating habits protect you from hunger pangs that make you reach out for the wrong foods. More important, regular food intake makes the body function more efficiently.

■ Do not go where you know you will find temptation. At weddings and parties, do not stand near the table laden with fattening food. At home, serve yourself in a *thali* and eat, rather than dipping into dishes just to taste, or just to finish that little bit of rice or *chapatti* or to give others company, or to finish left-overs, to finish a dish full of expensive ingredients, or to clean up your child's plate; the list is endless.

■ Eat slowly, take at least 20 minutes over your meal. It takes about that much time for the stomach to tell the brain it is no longer hungry. Chew slowly, at least 20 following various diet plans. According to him, frequent dieting gives the body starvation signals, and when food is once again available the body reacts by overstoring, being unable to differentiate between a weight loss regime and serious food deprivation. He further says that the rate of the breakdown of food is considerably reduced while dieting, as this is one of the survival tactics the body uses when food is scarce. This sluggish metabolism makes weight loss more difficult.

times and savour each mouthful. It will give you greater satisfaction from your food.

■ Weigh yourself regularly on the same weighing scale. Don't fool yourself that a few kilos here or there is not much. Think of the stuff you buy in the market. 5 kilos is a lot of weight

■ Do not talk about your efforts to change your food habits, as people will try and talk you out of it. If you are a compulsive eater, keep the right kind of snacks around; *moong* sprouts, boiled potatoes, carrots, cucumber, seasonal fruits, *channa*.

■ Learn to drink plain, clean sparkling water instead of tea, coffee, sherbets, colas, etc. Set yourself a goal as to what weight you want to achieve. Then work towards it steadily. Do not encourage people to pamper you with food.

■ There is an interesting book called *Dieting Makes You Fat* (London,1984), by Geoffery Cannon. The author has spent dozens of years of his life

■ Constant yet moderate eating habits, with occasional indulgences on weekends, is the best path to try and follow. It is a good idea to consult an expert on nutrition to chalk out a diet for you in accordance with your taste and preferences. Nutrition experts can be found in Home Science colleges, hospitals and nursing homes and in weight reduction clinics. They take into account your lifestyle. Do you cook and do other housework or are you physically inactive? They will consider whether you are pregnant, feeding the baby, or are just a simple housewife? Are you a vegetarian or a non-vegetarian? Taking all these factors into account, a diet chart will be made up specially for you.

■ And lastly, if you are putting on weight in leaps and bounds, although you are not eating much, get yourself checked by a doctor for any physical problem like malfunction of the thyroid gland.

# 6. Some Simple Exercises

During pregnancy, certain exercises should be done, keeping in mind the limitations and the needs of the pregnant body. The following exercises are recommended.

## STEP 1

Sit cross legged on a firm surface, be it a carpet, *dari* and/or blanket. As you sit cross-legged, become aware of the areas of your body that are touching the ground.

## STEP 2

Now imagine that you are a plant, and from the areas of your body that are touching the ground, imagine that there are roots growing down into the ground.

Your backbone is like a stem that rises straight and strong out of the ground.

Your head on the top is like a flower on the top of the stem and it reaches up towards the sun. Feel the top of your head reach up without raising your chin.

## STEP 3

Breathe in slowly and deeply the nourishment from the roots straight up to your head and slowly exhale. Imagine you are exhaling all your tensions with your breath.

Do this for 2 minutes.

## Grounding

*This exercise will help you sit up straight in the correct posture to do your exercises. It will also calm you and quieten your mind before you start your exercise regimen.*

81

## Neck Exercise

*In order to mobilise and strengthen the neck and shoulder muscles, the following exercises are helpful.*
*It also helps relieve tension in the neck and shoulder muscles.*

STEP 1 : Sit cross-legged with the back straight. Keep the head and the neck in one straight line.

STEP 2: Incline the head slightly downwards, so that the chin moves towards the chest.

STEP 3: Then straighten the head again and take it backwards with your mouth open, so that you are looking at the ceiling. Close your mouth, feeling the stretch in front of the neck and hold the position for a count of 6.

STEP 4: Bring the head back to starting position.

Do this 3 times.

## Shoulder Rotation

*Good for the upper back. This exercise helps relieve pain in the upper back and nape of the neck.*

STEP 1 : Sit cross-legged with the back straight. Keep the head and neck in a straight line.

STEP 2: Bring shoulders forward.

STEP 3: Raise shoulders up to your ears.

STEP 4: Thrust shoulders backwards, so that chest juts outwards.

STEP 5: Bring shoulders back to starting position.

STEP 6: Repeat these movements in one fluid motion, so that you make a circle with your shoulders.

STEP 7: Make circles in the opposite direction.

Do 5 circles in each direction.

## Deep Breathing

*This is not a simple exercise. You are exercising all the muscles of your carriage. It provides a lot of oxygen to you and your baby. Besides, when you breathe in, the diaphragm presses on the abdominal organs, massaging and invigorating them.*

POSITION
Sit cross-legged with the back straight. Keep the head and neck in a straight line.

STEP 1: Take a short breath in, then exhale slowly through pursed lips, to the maximum.

STEP 2: Let your lungs naturally fill up with air when exhalation is complete.

STEP 3: Breathe normally for about 3 breaths.

STEP 4: Repeat the first 3 steps.

Do this 3 times.

It is best to do this exercise early in the morning near plants (since when the sun shines, plants make oxygen). Moreover, exposure to the morning sun makes Vitamin D which helps in calcium absorption. There is also less dust and vehicle exhaust in the atmosphere at that time.

## Bust Exercise

*Exercises the pectoral muscles and helps lift and firm the breasts.*

STEP1 : Sit cross-legged with the back straight and keep your head and neck in a straight line.

STEP 2: Join both palms together under the breasts like a namaste away from the body in a flat position, that is, with the fingertips pointing straight ahead.

83

STEP 3: Press the palms firmly together and hold to a count of 10.

STEP 4: Release pressure on both palms.

STEP 5: Repeat 3 times.

STEP 6: Join both palms together like a namaste, in front of the breasts, away fom the body, in a slanting position.

STEP 7: Press the palms firmly together and hold to a count of 10.

STEP 8: Release pressure on both the palms.

STEP 9: Repeat 3 times.

STEP 10: Join both palms together like a namaste, with the fingertips pointing to your chin, yet not touching your body.

STEP 11: Press palms firmly together and hold to a count of 10.

STEP 12: Release pressure on both palms.

STEP 13: Repeat this 3 times.

## Pelvic Floor Exercise

*The pelvic floor muscles support the womb. They help to hold the extra weight of the growing uterus in pregnancy. Exercising these muscles helps to strengthen them and maintains their shape.*

POSITION

Sit cross-legged. Can also be done while standing or lying down. Start with Exercise A. After 3 days start Exercise B. After 3 more days graduate to Exercise C.

*Exercise A*

STEP 1: Exhale. Leave your pelvic floor absolutely relaxed, as when passing urine.

STEP 2: Now imagine that you interrupt or stop the flow

of urine for a while, by a slight contraction of the muscles.

STEP 3: Repeat the above steps 3 times.

*Exercise B*

The pelvic floor muscles are used during this exercise.

STEP 1: Exhale. Relax the pelvic floor.

STEP 2: Imagine that you want to pass urine badly, but you are at a public toilet and have to wait in the queue; and as you wait, you have to control the passing of urine by a strong contraction of your muscles.

STEP 3: Hold the contraction till a count of 6 and release.

Exhale and repeat the contraction twice.

> *An Exercise for Every Woman*
>
> Women need to do this exercise always. Beginning in pregnancy for the rest of their lives. Done mildly after delivery (exercise B) promotes healing. After healing is complete do exercise C. It helps regain the pre–pregnant tightness of these muscles.
>
> In the middle years around age forty when a woman exercises her pelvic floor muscles they remain strong and support the uterus. If they sag and lose their ability to support the uterus, an operation may be performed for a prolapsed uterus.

Your anus might also contract slightly, that does not matter, since your anus, vagina, and urethra are in one band of muscles. You might feel a slight tightening above the pubic hairline. You should not feel a tightening around the navel of your abdomen. If you do, it is a sign that you should locate the contraction backwards towards the anus instead. You are now ready for the final step of the exercise.

*Exercise C*

STEP 1: Exhale.

STEP 2: Contract your pelvic floor muscles a little bit. Count to 6.

STEP 3: Contract your pelvic floor muscles a little more. Count to 6.

> *Precautions*
>
> **Always exhale before starting this exercise.**

STEP 4: Contract your pelvic floor muscles the
maximum you can. Count to 6.

STEP 5: Exhale slowly and gently release or
let go of your pelvic floor muscles, while you
exhale.

STEP 6: Breathe normally for 3 to 4 breaths.

Repeat. Do this exercise 5 times.

If you develop an ache in the muscles, it is because
these muscles are not used to being exercised. The
pain is like the pain you would get in your arm if you
played badminton after many days. So do not stop
the exercise, but do it in one continuous contraction
to the count of 6, instead.

Repeat at least 5 times.

## Ankle Movements

*This exercise has its base in yoga. It exercises the ankles, a
part of the body not generally exercised. It feels good, since the
strain of the extra weight of pregnancy is carried by this area of
the body.*

STEP 1: Sit with one leg outstretched, the other leg
bent at the knee, and the lower part of the bent leg
(just above the ankle) resting on the thigh of the
outstretched leg.
Rest your back against the wall if you like.

STEP 2: Hold the bent leg just above the ankle with
one hand; and with the other hand rotate the foot
from the ankle.

STEP 3: Rotate the foot 5 times clockwise
and 5 times anti-clockwise.

Repeat with the other leg.

## Mochi / Cobbler Pose

*Relaxes and stabilizes the pelvis. Exercises the pelvic joints. Also stretches the inner thigh and the pelvic floor muscles.*

STEP 1: Bring the soles of your feet together in front of you, so that you form a *namaste* with your feet.

STEP 2: Now, with your hands hold the soles of your feet together, and drag them inwards along the floor towards your body.
You will feel a stretch on your inner thigh.
Do once and stay in position as long as you comfortably can.

## Pelvic Lift

*Strengthens the back muscles and relieves lower backache or feeling of congestion in the groin.*

STEP 1: Lie down flat on your back. Bend both legs at knees and place feet on the floor.

STEP 2: Now put your weight on both feet and raise your hips off the floor.

STEP 3: Once raised, stay in position for at least 10 counts.

STEP 4: Then gently lower yourself back to the floor.

Do once or twice.

Help in lifting the pelvis may be taken

87

from someone if you are unable to do so independently. Someone can stand by your side next to your hips and place both arms around your lower back and help you rise off the floor.

## Knee Chest Position

*When you are upright all day, the organs hang from the spine as a flag hangs from a pole. When you position yourself for this exercise by going on all fours, the organs hang from the spine like clothes from a line. Hence this exercise relaxes the back.*

*When you do this exercise, the weight of the pregnant uterus is shifted away from the pelvic floor and the spine. It therefore takes care of backache and radiating pains in the hips and legs.*

*This exercise also feels good if you have a gastric problem and are wanting to burp to relieve yourself.*

STEP 1: Kneel on the floor with knees slightly apart. Then go forward on all fours, by placing your palms on the floor in front of you directly under your shoulder joint. Keep your head down and back straight. Keep your head down all the while. Raising the head will tend to encourage the hollowing or caving in of the back. If the back is allowed to hollow, it can give rise to a backache.

Stay for a while in this position.

STEP 2: Go down, putting your elbows in place of your palms, and point palms towards opposite elbows.

STEP 3: Rest your head on your arms. If your stomach pushes against the thighs, separate your knees further, so that your stomach fits in the hollow between your thighs. Secondly, guard against hollowing of the back. If hollowing occurs, correct it by gently pulling in your stomach.

STEP 4: Stay in position as long as you comfortably can. Breathe normally. While in position you will feel a rush of blood towards the face which will make your face warm. Do not worry.

> *Precaution*
>
> **If you have high blood pressure, stay in the all fours position but avoid getting the head down.**

This exercise is to be done once.
The longer the position is maintained, the greater the benefit derived from it.

## Leg Lift

*In pregnancy there is a tendency to form varicose veins in the legs. Varicose veins are dark looking veins that appear above or below the knees as a result of pooling of impure blood in the legs. Due to the congestion in the groin region impure blood cannot easily flow back to the heart for purification.*

*This exercise helps prevent varicose veins by assisting the blood to flow back towards the heart past the groin area. It soothes the legs.*

> *Precautions*
>
> **If you are prone to leg cramps, do not point your toe as you raise the leg. It will give you a cramp.**

STEP 1: Lie on your side with one arm stretched outwards under your head, and the palm of the other arm placed in front of you. Place a pillow between your abdomen and the floor.

STEP 2: Raise the upper leg higher than your hip.

STEP 3: Hold for a count of 6.

STEP 4: Gently bring back to the starting position.

Repeat 3 to 4 times with each leg.

## Curling Leaf

*Takes off the strain from the back while you are getting up and reduces the possibility of backache.*

STEP 1: Lie flat on your back. Bend the left leg at the knee, placing the foot next to the knee of the outstretched leg. Stretch the right arm behind your head.

STEP 2: Put the weight of your body on the foot of the bent left leg.

STEP 3: Roll your body in the opposite direction, that is, to the right.

STEP 3: Simultaneously, as you roll on to the right side, bring your left palm to rest on the floor, in front of your abdomen.

STEP 5: Now straighten your left leg and rise up with your weight supported by both palms.

Repeat with the other leg.

Practise 4 times till perfected. Then use simply as a way of getting up.

## Leg Swing

*There are 3 joints in the pelvis which spread slightly apart during delivery.*

*The present day lifestyle of sitting on chairs all the time makes these joints inflexible. This exercise is to make them flexible, by bringing some movement in them.*

POSITION
Stand with your hands on your hips and feet placed normally.

*Exercise A*

STEP 1: Tilt very slightly to the left side and swing the right leg forward and then backward 4 times.

STEP 2: Repeat with the other leg.

The swing forward and backward should not be exaggerated. About 1 foot forward and 1 foot backward is fine. Done overenthusiastically, it could cause an ache in the sacro-iliac joints that have already been softened by hormones in preparation for birth.

If you tend to lose balance, then pause, at the starting position between each forward and backward swing.

*Exercise B*

STEP 1: Stand with hands on hips.

STEP 2: Swing one leg outward sideways and bring back to the starting position. Repeat 3 times.

STEP 3 : Repeat with the other leg.

## Pelvic Tilting

*This exercise relieves lower backache and also helps retain abdominal tone, so that after your baby is born, the abdomen will tone up faster and more easily.*

*Your bony pelvic basin houses your reproductive organs like your ovaries and uterus. As the uterus balloons up with pregnancy, it spills out of the pelvic basin, putting its weight on the abdominal wall. The baby lies on the abdominal wall as though it were lying on a hammock. This weight on the abdominal wall puts pressure on the lower back muscles which begin to pain. It also causes the abdominal wall to stretch to its maximum and lose its tone and elasticity, giving rise to stretch marks.*

*This exercise tilts the pelvis in a way that the contents of the pelvis that press the abdominal wall are pushed inwards, so that their weight is taken by the bony pelvis during the duration of the exercise. This gives respite to the abdominal wall from stretching and relieves backache.*

### Exercise A

STEP 1: Stand normally.

STEP 2: Exhale.

STEP 3: Bend slightly at the knees.

STEP 4: Contract and tighten your bottom as if you are holding a hundred rupee note in your bottom! As you tighten your buttocks, and tense the muscles there, your pubic area in the front will be thrust forward and upward towards your navel. Your abdomen will be tilted backward towards your backbone. At the same time the curve in the middle of your back will straighten out.

STEP 5: Hold the position for a count of 6.

STEP 6: Release and go back to the starting position.

Repeat 5 times.

### Exercise B

If you are fairly advanced in pregnancy, you could do this exercise in a lying position.

STEP 1: Lie down flat on your

92

Bend legs at the knees and
place feet flat on the floor.

STEP 2: Place a folded hand towel
or napkin in the hollow of
your back.

STEP 3: Exhale or sigh out.

STEP 4: Tighten the buttock
muscles and draw in the lower
abdomen.

STEP 5: Simultaneously flatten the
hollow of your back against the floor and press on the
folded towel.

STEP 6: Hold for a count of 6.

STEP 7: Release and breathe normally.

Repeat this excercise 5 times.

## Walking for Cramps and Arches of the Foot

*Cramps can sometimes occur due to lack of blood circulation.
This exercise gives a boost to circulation of blood in your lower
limbs.*

STEP 1: Stand normally. You should have about 6 feet of
open space for walking.

STEP 2: Walk across the 6–foot space on
your toes.

STEP 3: Then walk back on your heels.

STEP 4: Finally walk on the outer sider of
your feet.

Do once every day before bedtime.

Sometimes cramps can also occur due to lack of
calcium, Vitamin B or E. If cramps do not get
alleviated with walking, check your
diet.

## Squatting

*While squatting, the pelvic inlet, outlet, and canal are at
their widest. Those using the squatting type toilet are at an
advantage as it exercises your joints and muscles without
having to do much. Use it more frequently if you have one in
the house.*

*Squatting correctly positions the growing baby and the uterus.
It also cures constipation.*

STEP 1: Squat as when using an Indian toilet. If you are
well advanced in pregnancy, with a big stomach,
follow these steps:

STEP 2: Stand normally, with your bottom touching
the wall.

STEP 3: Now rise on your toes.

STEP 4: Go down into a squat.

STEP 5: Do not go into a complete squat, remain in a
slightly raised position.

STEP 6: Rest your lower back against the wall, and
spread your knees as wide apart as you can.

STEP 7: Stay for at least 2 minutes in the final
position.

STEP 8: Now go forward on your hands and then
your knees to come out of the squatting
position.

In the 9th month when the baby is in a head-down
position, in order to encourage the fixing or the
engagement of the baby's head, instead of squatting, one
could sit with knees bent and a couple of cushions on
one's calves.

This position would cause the pelvic structure to be
raised to above the level of the knees, with a forward
tilt to it, so that the angle becomes perfect for the baby
to enter the pelvic inlet. This position called 'Optimal

94

Foetal Positioning' was advocated by Jean Sutton and Pauline Scott, midwife and childbirth educator from New Zealand. It can be adopted by a woman as she watches TV or when she is sitting on the bed.

> **Precaution**
>
> Squatting should not be done by a woman who has had a stitch put on the mouth of the uterus by the doctor, nor by one who is bleeding in pregnancy, or who is on bed rest because of a low-lying placenta.
>
> Squatting should also be avoided in case of severe or painful varicose veins or piles.

## Aum Breathing

*This exercise has its base in yoga and is relaxing both to the mother and the baby. (Source : Swami Satyanand, Bihar School of Yoga)*

STEP 1: Sit cross-legged with the back straight. Keep the head and neck in a straight line.

Place you thumbs firmly on the small triangular flap before the ear orifice. In this way you will block out any distraction caused by surrounding sounds.

Place the 2 fingers after your thumb lightly on your eyes.

Place the next 2 fingers one above and one below the lips.

STEP 2: Breathe in.

STEP 3: As you breathe out or exhale say the word *Aum*.

Repeat 5 times without a break.

If while doing this exercise you feel breathless, take a pause by taking a sigh, that is, a deep inhalation and exhalation, in between the *Aum* breaths.

## Relaxation

It is very important for a woman to remain as relaxed as she can through pregnancy. A good time to practise relaxation is when you know you are not going to need to rush off in 10 minutes, when all your work is done, when you do not expect to be called or made to answer the telephone or door bell.

Lie down quietly and allow your mind and body 5 to 10 minutes to quieten down. Use this time to also shift around and find a comfortable position to relax in, taking cushions, pillows, sheets or blankets as required. Once settled, allow your thoughts to pour in. Close your eyes and watch your thoughts in a detached way, as though you are watching a movie on the screen. Be detached: do not judge your thoughts; simply watch them for about 10 to 15 minutes.

 Now try to do some conscious relaxation. Tape the following relaxation and play it to yourself or have someone read it to you:

Relax the toes, feet and ankles.
Relax the nerves that hold the muscles of my toes, feet and ankles.
Relax my calves.
Relax the nerves that hold the muscles of my calves.
Relax my knees.
Relax the nerves that hold the muscles of my knees.
Relax my thighs.
Relax the nerves that hold the muscles of my thighs.
Now my lower limbs are relaxed and will not get unrelaxed.

Relax my pelvic floor.

Relax the nerves that hold the muscles of my pelvic floor.

Relax my buttocks.

Relax the nerves that hold the muscles of my buttocks.

Relax my womb and my lower abdomen.

Relax the nerves that hold the muscles of my lower abdomen.

Now my lower abdomen is relaxed and will not get unrelaxed.

Relax my back.

Relax my shoulder blades.

Relax the nerves that hold the muscles of my back.

Now my back is relaxed and will not get unrelaxed.

Relax my upper arms.

Relax my lower arms.

Relax my palms and fingers.

Relax the nerves that hold the muscles of my arms.

Now my arms are relaxed and will not get unrelaxed.

Relax my neck.

Relax the nerves that hold the muscles of my neck.

Now my neck is relaxed and will not get unrelaxed.

Relax my chin and face.

Relax the nerves that hold the muscles of my chin and face.

Now my face is relaxed and will not get unrelaxed.

Relax the top of my head.

Relax the back of my head.

Relax the nerves that hold the muscles of my head.

Now my head is relaxed and will not get unrelaxed.

Now relaxation is seeping into my brain.

Relax the nerves that hold the muscles of my brain.

Now my brain is relaxed and will not get unrelaxed.

Keep lying down with your eyes closed.

After relaxation do not get up suddenly. First become aware of your surroundings. Remember the room in which you are lying, and the furniture/doors/windows in it. Slowly move your hands and feet.

Rise gently.

# A Prayer

Go Placidly
Amid the Noise and Haste
And remember what peace there
may be in silence.

As far as possible without surrender
be on good terms with all persons.

Speak your truth quietly and
clearly: and listen to others.

Even the dull and ignorant; they
too have their story.

Avoid loud and aggressive persons,
they are vexations to the spirit.

If you compare yourself with others,
you may become vain and bitter;

For always there will be greater and
lesser persons than yourself.

Enjoy your achievements as well as
your plans.

Keep interested in your own career,
however humble;

It is a real possession in the
changing fortunes of time.

Exercise caution in your business
affairs;

For the world is full of trickery.

But let this not blind you to what
virtue there is;

Many persons strive for high ideals;

And everywhere life is full of
heroism.

Be yourself. Especially, do not feign
affection.

Neither be cynical about love; for in
the face of all aridity and
disenchantment, it is perennial as
the grass.

Take kindly the counsel of the years,
gracefully surrendering the things
of youth.

Nurture strength of spirit to shield
you in sudden misfortune.

But do not distress yourself with
imaginings.

Many fears are born of fatigue and
loneliness.

Beyond a wholesome discipline, be
gentle with yourself.

You are a child of the universe; no
less than the trees and the stars; you
have a right to be here. And whether
or not it is clear to you,

no doubt the universe is unfolding
as it should.

Therefore be at peace with God,
whatever you conceive Him to be,

And whatever your labours and
aspirations, in the noisy confusion
of life.

Keep peace with your soul.

With all its sham, drudgery and
broken dreams,

It is still a beautiful world.

Be careful.
Strive to be happy.

Found in Old Saint Paul's Church, Baltimore, 1692

# 7. Sex During Pregnancy

Sex in pregnancy is perfectly normal. In fact it can bring a new delight with it since contraception is out of the way. However, if you have previously lost a baby, been treated for infertility, or miscarried, the doctor may tell you to avoid sex when your period would have been due, or generally. If you have been asked to avoid intercourse, you can always indulge in caressing, stroking, etc. Do not feel shy to ask the doctor how long you have to avoid intercourse, since doctors may forget to say when you are past the time you are likely to miscarry. You may be asked to avoid intercourse if you have had an earlier premature labour.

If you are under great strain at work, or if you are worried about the financial responsibility of having a baby, or if you are angry about being pregnant, then you may not desire or enjoy lovemaking.

Some women feel inclined towards sex in pregnancy, while others do not. A woman's feeling should be respected. When making love certain considerations have to be kept in mind, like the growing abdomen or the increased sensitivity of the breasts. Different positions can be experimented with, in accordance with whatever is comfortable.

Men often fear that during intercourse they may in some way harm the baby. You cannot hurt the baby during intercourse. The baby is protected by the water bag and the water around it. The water acts as a shock absorber to protect the baby from accidental blows or jerks. The uterus is housed in the bony framework of the pelvic bones, which provide protection. In the mouth of the womb, called the cervix, is a plug of mucus which seals the womb and prevents infection from entering the womb.

If a woman is overly anxious about her pregnancy, and her husband shares her anxiety, they will together make each other more tense. They may be so afraid of sexual arousal that they may not even lovingly touch and feel each other. A perpetual state of tension is not going to help matters. Stress of any kind is to be avoided in pregnancy. Both partners need to relax. Stroking and massaging the tension away is a good idea. Do it to each other in turns.

# Bleeding

Bleeding in early pregnancy may be caused if the level of your pregnancy hormone is not sufficiently high to stop your period. Such bleeding is slight, occurs for a month or a few months, when your period would have been due. It is slight with a darkish discharge, for an hour, a day or two, and there is no pain. The true significance of bleeding at the time of the period is not clear. Many women who experience it otherwise have a perfectly normal pregnancy, and a perfectly healthy baby.

However, any bleeding which occurs during pregnancy is considered a threatened abortion, and the doctor's advice must be sought. When a threatened abortion occurs, the bleeding is usually bright red or pink, which signifies that the loss is from within the uterus. When the bleeding stops, the vaginal discharge changes to dark red or brown. Normally bed rest is continued until 3 days after the brown discharge has stopped.

A threatened abortion most commonly occurs during the first three suppressed periods, that is, in the first

3 months or the 4th, 8th or 12th week of pregnancy. It could also occur in the 14th week, when the placenta takes over the production of hormones from the ovaries.

In case of threatened abortion, the doctor will advise immediate bed rest. A woman is allowed to get up only to go to the toilet. She must stay quietly in bed. She should use sanitary towels, which should be changed frequently and saved for the doctor to examine. A threatened abortion indicates an unstable pregnancy and care should be taken to rest when a period would have been due. Sexual intercourse should not take place until the doctor permits it (*see p.56*).

The penis in the vagina is not threatening as commonly believed. It is more the contractions of the uterus which are triggered off when a woman reaches orgasm that can be followed by further contractions. If you are ready to start labour or about to miscarry, these contractions may set off labour.

## Intercourse

It therefore follows that if your delivery is overdue this may be a more pleasant way of starting labour than a glucose drip given with a synthetic hormone added to it. Also, semen contains prostaglandin hormones which may cause the uterus to contract, or its mouth, the cervix, to soften. The greater the penetration of the penis during intercourse, the closer it will get to the cervix and bathe it with semen. It would be a good idea to place a pillow under your hips during intercourse. After your partner has ejaculated he should stay inside for a few minutes and the position must be maintained so that the prostaglandin hormone in the semen reaches the cervix. You should delay washing yourself by 10 to 15 minutes. Keep lying with the pillow under your hips.

From intercourse or from masturbation if you have an orgasm, it causes 5 to 15 contractions, and these may be sufficient to induce labour. If you are not ready to go into labour, the effects of an orgasm in a normal stable pregnancy are not known. However, it has been suggested that when a woman reaches orgasm or a climax, and her uterus contracts, the fetus may get extra blood from the congested blood vessels.

Ordinarily uterine contractions are quite common. They occur every few minutes throughout a woman's reproductive life from puberty to menopause, without being felt. Unless a woman is at the end of her pregnancy, unless her cervix is ready or she has a history of premature birth, uterine contractions during intercourse will not cause premature labour *(see p.137)*.

## Breast Stimulation

Breast stimulation can also help start labour if your body and your baby are ready for the birth, so you need not worry about it starting labour prematurely. Stimulation of the breasts brings about contractions of the uterus, since it produces a powerful endocrine hormone by the pituitary gland, called oxytocin. A synthetic form of the same hormone in much larger doses is used by doctors to stimulate labour. If you have a tendency to start labour prematurely, avoid breast stimulation.

Breast stimulation during labour speeds up the process of labour, and in pregnancy assists in the effacement of the cervix or mouth of the womb, whereby it thins out, and softens or ripens, in preparation for birth. If a woman's delivery is overdue and labour is induced by an intravenous drip, the labour has greater chances of ending in a normal delivery if the cervix has been softened and thinned out. Hence with breast stimulation an induced labour is more likely to end up in a normal delivery rather than in a Caesarean section. On the other hand it may even stimulate labour to start spontaneously (see p. 137).

## After the Birth

After the birth of the baby you will have a longish period lasting a week or several weeks. Then, if you are breastfeeding you may not have a period for several months. Even though you do not have a period, you can still conceive and become pregnant. It is therefore advisable to use a contraceptive when you resume intercourse. You can resume intercourse after 40 days or 6 weeks, since it takes that much time for the vagina to heal. You can use a lubricant like vaseline the first few times. You must consult your doctor as to which contraceptive you should use. Should intercourse take place earlier, a contraceptive like the condom can be used (see p. 176).

# 8. Labour Time

There are 3 signs that could herald the onset of labour. These may appear by themselves or 2 may even appear together approximately 15 days before the expected date of delivery or after.

You may notice a thick mucus discharge which could be white, pink or brown in colour. Sometimes the mucus may even contain some amount of bright red blood mixed in it.

*Mucus Discharge or the show*

The discharge occurs from the mouth of the womb or cervix which is plugged with mucus to prevent infection from entering the womb.

A week or so before labour begins, the cervix can thin out and flatten. As this happens, the mucus plug escapes and you notice a thick lumpy mucus discharge. This discharge is a sign that your body is getting ready for the birth process. It is no cause for alarm.

The doctor would say that your cervix is now ripe, ready, or effaced.

The muscular contractions of the uterus are felt as periodic discomfort, and often referred to as pain. Initially contractions are mild. They may feel like the mild discomfort felt at the beginning of a menstrual period. Or one may mistake them for discomfort that accompanies an upset stomach, since it is not uncommon to have diarrhoea before labour begins. On some occasions women feel it is discomfort arising from tight clothing around the waist. However, even when you switch to more comfortable clothing or lighter food, the discomfort persists. It comes and goes periodically.

*Contractions*

When you realise this, begin to make a note of the time whenever the discomfort occurs. If you find it occurring half-hourly, you know it is real labour. It could also occur more frequently, for example, every 15 minutes. So, when it occurs at fixed intervals, you know it is real labour.

Sometimes, before labour begins you feel practice contractions or false contractions. These are contractions of the uterus in preparation for birth. Practice contractions feel similar to real contractions, but they occur at irregular intervals.

So while practice contractions have a haphazard interval between them, real contractions will have fixed, rhythmical intervals.

It is possible that after starting at periodic intervals, contractions might stop for a day or so, only to restart later. There is no harm if contractions stop. There is, at times, a slowly unfolding labour that starts and stops on and off, until it gets properly established. So you can safely stay at home until your contractions get to be 10 minutes apart. Once they are timed every 10 minutes, they are properly established and less likely to stop.

Do not panic if contractions start at 5 minute intervals.

Contractions may stop for a while when you check into the strange atmosphere of the hospital or nursing home. If that happens, just walk around and get familiar with the place. See where the toilet is, where the nursing station is, the position of your room on the floor where you are. Stroll in the corridor and your contractions will start again as you get familiar with your environment. You could also go and have a look at the nursing home or hospital earlier, while pregnant.

After 10 minute intervals the contractions will shift to 5 minute intervals and for a short while before birth, to every 2 minutes. During birth again the interval will become 5 minutes.

The baby is encased in the amniotic sac. Sometimes the amniotic sac bursts and all the amniotic water gushes out, as though a tap were opened inside you at full blast. The amniotic sac may burst before labour begins. It could happen at any time in the 9th month, but it mostly happens at night. So you could spread a rubber sheet or rubber cloth across the middle of your bed. It can be bought from a chemist or a cloth shop. (It is called *momjama* in Hindi).

When this happens, the amniotic fluid also sweeps out the mucus plug on its way out. The protection of the

*Fluid leak*

---

### When Urgent Medical Attention is Needed

**A Coloured Trickle**

The trickle that appears from the amniotic sac is usually clear. But if the trickle appears muddy or greenish and has a foul smell, you must get in touch with your doctor immediately. The colour in the amniotic fluid comes if the baby passes stool inside the womb, which it normally does after birth.

So, once you have what is called meconium staining of the amniotic fluid you need to be under medical observation. If, along with meconium staining, there is an adverse effect on the baby's heart rate (the normal heart rate is 120 to 160 beats per minute), it would indicate a need for a Caesarean section. If the fetal heart rate is not affected, labour can progress normally, culminating in a normal delivery.

**Bright Red Bleeding**

If you experience bright, fresh, red bleeding like when you cut your finger, or as at the height of a period, you should be in touch with your doctor immediately.

Bright, fresh, red bleeding occurs if there is placenta previa, a condition in which the placenta lies between the baby's head and the mouth of the uterus, blocking the baby's exit.

Or, it could occur if the placenta, the organ that nourishes the baby, detaches or peels away from the wall of the uterus . If a small portion has peeled away, it may be quite harmless, but nevertheless you will have to be under observation, to make sure it does not adversely affect the heartbeat of the baby. The normal heartbeat of the baby in labour would fluctuate between 120 and 160 beats per minute. Below 120, or above 160 are both considered fetal distress. Occasionally, a few drops of blood may escape a couple of days after intercourse or a vaginal examination by the doctor. This is quite harmless.

plug and the amniotic fluid is now absent. For this reason, the woman is now more susceptible to infection each time an internal examination is given. So, once the water bag bursts, doctors like to deliver the baby within 24 hours.

The common practice is to put a woman whose water bag has burst on a drip of glucose to which a synthetic hormone called syntocinon has been added in order to trigger off contractions artificially.

However, if you wait 4 to 5 hours before fixing a drip, it is possible that contractions may start spontaneously, on their own and thus eliminate the need of a drip. It would be more pleasant if this happened, since spontaneous contractions are gentler than contractions that are artificially induced.

So, if the water bag bursts, you check into a hospital, but request for the drip to be delayed by 4 to 5 hours. It is a simple request. Keeping in mind that the baby should arrive within 24 hours, waiting 4 to 5 hours still leaves an ample period of 19 to 20 hours for the birth.

On some occasions the amniotic sac may not burst, but might just trickle instead. The trickle will be clear and uncontrollable. Wear a sanitary pad and take rest at home.

After some time the amniotic sac might seal itself and the trickle might stop. It might recur after some time, or it might be followed by contractions.

Go to the hospital when the contractions are 10 minutes apart, or if the trickle gets out of control and cannot be contained by a sanitary pad. The sanitary pad should be changed often to avoid infection.

# Positions to Adopt in Labour

Once labour begins, it is best to be upright rather than lying down flat on your back. Upright would mean walking/kneeling/standing and other positions we shall discuss shortly. Being upright in labour gives the following advantages:

- The force of gravity helps in the descent of the baby. (The force of gravity is constantly pulling down things.)
  The baby with its own weight will descend through the birth canal sooner when the mother is upright, rather than when she is lying down.
- When the mother lies flat on her back, a blood vessel gets compressed by the weight of the uterus and the baby on the one hand and the backbone on the other. This hampers the blood flow to and from the heart, and increases the chance of distress in the mother and the baby.
- Being upright lifts the compression on the blood vessel, so that the blood flow to the mother and the baby is more efficient and both are therefore more alert and awake during birth.
- When the mother is lying down, the vagina is at upward slant, so the baby has an uphill task before it. When the mother is upright, e.g. standing, it becomes a downward descent for the baby.
- During birth the head of the baby passes first the top brim of the pelvic basin and then the bottom outlet of the pelvic basin. Forming part of the outlet at the bottom of the pelvis is the tail bone. The tail bone is a flexible bone. If you do not lie or sit on it while in labour, it moves away as the baby comes through the outlet of the pelvis, and the space for the baby's exit

increases by as much as 30%.

■ In 1977, a study in Birmingham Maternity Hospital compared a group of women who walked about during labour, with a group that lay down horizontally through most of labour. The results showed that in women who walked about during labour,

(i) the duration of labour was shorter;

(ii) there was less need for painkillers;

(iii) the incidence of fetal heart abnormalities was markedly smaller; and

(iv) they experienced less pain.

■ Further studies have revealed that:

### Precaution

There is just one instance when it is better for you to lie down rather than be upright.

At about 36 weeks, the head of the baby fixes in the brim of the pelvic basin. In some instances, the head does not lower and fix in the pelvic basin, but remains floating above the pelvic inlet. This is called a floating head. Fairly often, a floating head fixes in the pelvic basin after labour begins.

In the last month of pregnancy when you go for weekly check ups to your doctor, ask if the baby's head has fixed or engaged. If you have a floating head and the water bag bursts, it is possible that as all the water drains out, the umbilical cord may also be swept downwards with the water and come to lie between the baby's head and brim of the bony pelvic basin. In this case, if you remain upright, you may cause the cord to be squashed between the baby's head and the pelvis, a most undersirable situation, medically called cord prolapse. It is through the cord that the baby receives oxygen and nourishment.

When there is the rare combination of floating of the baby's head and the bursting of the water bag, you must remain lying down or adopt the knee-chest position, or go into the all fours position.

(i) the strength or intensity of contractions is greater when women are moving about in labour; and

(ii) there is greater regularity and frequency of contractions.

## Upright Position for Labour

Walking is the best position for labour. You can walk about your room, at a relaxed leisurely pace. Avoid brisk walking; it will tire you out. Stroll about, and when your contraction is felt:

*Walking*

- Stop walking. Stand where you are, with your feet nicely apart, to take the even distribution of your weight. Place both palms on your lower abdomen. Make a circular rotating movement with your hips, during the duration of your contraction. When the contraction is over, you can resume walking.

- If you happen to be near a wall when a contraction is felt, stop walking. Stand facing the wall. Place your feet nicely apart, about 6 inches away from the wall. Place your palms on the wall at shoulder level. Keeping your body straight, bring it slightly forward by bending elbows, then push back with your palms. Keep up this gentle forward and backward movement while the contraction lasts. Avoid jutting the stomach forward and increasing the curve of your back, as this can lead to backache.
If you do not find the forward and backward movement comfortable, you can instead make circles with your hips.

DO

AVOID

- Alternatively, while you stand facing the wall, place

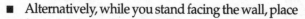

111

your feet a little away from the wall, with raised arms bent at the elbow on the wall, and use them to rest your forehead on. This position helps to make the contraction stronger, especially beneficial if contractions are weak.

When the contraction passes, resume walking.

*A bin, in case the water bag bursts*

In case the water bag bursts, and all the water gushes out altogether, the uterus is emptied of one litre of fluid. However, the water bag carries on making water which collects in the uterus and is expelled during a contraction. This would cause water running down your legs in case you are standing, or water wetting your bed in case you are sitting on a bed. In case you are walking, to avoid wetness, you could sit on a waste bin so that the water drips into the bin and you are left dry. Alternatively you could sit on a bed pan if you are on the bed. Or, ask for a chair with a commode.

*Using a dining chair*

If you have labour at night when you are a bit sleepy, or if you are tired and do not want to walk or stand, this position can be used.

A dining chair is used, since it narrows on the back and has no arms. Sit facing the back of the chair, with legs on either side (as you would sit when riding a horse). Use the back to rest your head.

As you lean forward to rest your head on the back of the chair, your tail bone lifts off and moves away from the pelvic outlet, making room for the baby.

When you are tired of walking, you can

112

switch to kneeling. You could kneel on the
hospital bed.

Place a soft thick pillow on the back of your legs,
that is, on the calves. Sit on the thick pillow when you
are not having a contraction. When a contraction is
felt, rise up on your knees, hold the headboard or
footboard and bend forward or make rotating circles
with your hips.

*Kneeling*

Resume sitting when the contraction passes.

# Backache in Labour

If you feel most of the discomfort of your contraction
on your lower back, you are experiencing back
labour. Back labour would mean that the baby is
posterior, that is, instead of facing the mother's
backbone, it is facing the mother's abdomen. The back
of the baby's head puts pressure on the mother's
backbone, causing a low backache. Counterpressure
on the lower back will relieve the discomfort.

*Standing
with back to
wall*

You will feel comfortable if you stand with your
back to the wall and press the part of the back that
hurts, against the wall. To get maximum pressure on
the lower back, you can hunch your shoulders
forward.

In case of a backache and posterior baby this position helps relieve the backache and guide the baby to an anterior position.

It also slows down fast labour.

First kneel with your knees one foot apart. Place your hands in front of you and go into the all fours position. Rotate the hip in circles.

# When on the Drip

The drip implies that glucose drips from a bottle through a tube, straight into your vein, through a needle that is inserted in your arm. The bottle of glucose is attached sometimes to a rod at the side of the bed; and sometimes to a rod attached to a stand with wheels (*see p. 135*).

*Sitting on the bed*

If the drip is fixed to the side of your bed, you have to remain in bed. Instead of lying down, you can adjust your bed in a sitting position.

When contraction occurs, lean forward, cross your legs and place the arm free of the drip, on the bed in front of you. Do your breathing. When the contraction is gone, sit back again and close your eyes and relax until the next contraction.

Alternatively you can get off the bed and sit on a chair in front of the bed or stand in front of the bed. When the contraction comes, you can stand, hold the edge of the bed for support with your free hand.

114

As you stand like this, if you like, you can also move your hips in circular motion.

# Comforters

Placing the palms on the lower abdomen and lower back of a woman who is having a contraction is of immense comfort to the labouring woman.

*Palming*

Just behind the muscles of the lower abdomen, the uterus contracts vigorously during a contraction. On the lower back, the joints of the pelvic structure spread apart at birth. Hence placing of palms on these two areas soothes the mother. It could be practised along with any position of labour.

Often a woman in labour desires to hold on to something or someone very tightly. If you have this urge, your partner should hold your palm with a firm, tight pressure. You should avoid gripping your partner's hand, so that you do not waste energy and strength while doing so; and you do not tense your body. Remove rings before trying this, they could hurt.

*Hand squeeze*

Your partner's thumb should be placed at the back of your hand. The remaining 4 fingers should fold on the back of the hand from the opposite side. The grip should be firm. You should tell your partner if you want to increase the pressure or have it lessened.

The skin and muscles of the abdomen are very tense during a uterine contraction. A light massage or

*Effleurage*

115

brushing will lessen this tension.

Effleurage is a light moving of your fingertips on your lower abdomen, that is, between the navel and the pubic hair. Place the fingertips of both hands on either side of the navel. Make circles by moving fingers lightly in a circular motion from the centre of the abdomen, outwards, towards the hips. Then down towards the pubic hairline and up towards the navel.

If you are on the drip and one hand is immobilised, you can massage with the fingertips of one hand, from side to side; that is, from one hip to the other, across the lower abdomen. Your partner could do this massage for you.

The fingertips should move in light strokes, rubbing should be avoided. The lighter the strokes, the better. It should be done simultaneously with breathing exercise. Apply talcum powder as needed.

*Leg massage*

If you feel your legs are weak or shaky, a massage firmly up from above the ankles, on the sides of your legs, will feel good. You can use talcum powder so that your fingers run smoothly and are not hampered by perspiration.

If you feel shaky on the thighs, this massage can be done from above the knees, on the inner and outer sides of the thighs. Sometimes this massage could be done after the birth of the baby.

## For a Backache

In labour, a slight discomfort in the back is common. Backache is more pronounced in the case of back labour or a posterior baby, when the discomfort of labour is concentrated more in the lower back than in the lower abdomen.

Lie on your side. Take a pillow under your head and another pillow between your knees.

*Back massage*

Your partner should sit facing your back. With one hand he can hold your hip, so that you do not have to brace yourself, and with the other hand, locate the flat, hard surface of your lower back, just above your hips. Once located, the heel of the palm should be pressed on the spot, and once pressed, rotate it clockwise and anti–clockwise. This massage can be practised during pregnancy too, in case of a backache.

Since a great amount of pressure is applied by the palm, it helps the person massaging, to support the elbow of the hand on the thigh. However, if tiredness sets in, your partner can instead sit back–to–back with you.

You should continue lying on your side, as for the back massage. Your partner should sit against your lower back, as close as he/she can get, with his/her back straight. That is, leaning on you should be avoided, or else you will feel that you might tumble over.

*Back to back*

At times, if your partner is male, just this sitting is adequate. However, if you feel the pressure is less, your partner should lean

117

forward, cross both palms at the back, place them on your lower back and straighten again. This will add to the pressure and bring greater comfort.

You can guide your partner as to where exactly you would like the pressure, higher, lower, or a little to the side.

*Tennis ball*

A tennis ball can be effectively used to massage your lower back. To use a tennis ball, you must have a foam mattress. It cannot be used on a cotton or coir foam mattress.

Lie down on a foam mattress, placing a tennis ball between your lower back and the mattress. The tennis ball will massage your lower back as you lie on it. It will bring comfort for 15 to 20 minutes.

The tennis ball could also be used in a standing position. Stand straight against the wall. Balance the ball between your back and the wall, you could place the ball on your upper or lower back, wherever there is pain. Move from side to side so that the ball massages you.

During a contraction stand and have your partner place one hand on your lower abdomen, just above the pubic hairline, and the other hand should be placed on the lower back, above the hips. No pressure is required to be given with the hands. The hands are to be placed gently on these two places.

After a contraction, with both hands in place, exhale, then let go of your abdomen. Relax your abdomen towards the hand. Relax your pelvic floor. Leave the pelvic floor relaxed as though you are passing urine. Imagine your pelvis is opening up, and having passed through it your baby is now coming through your relaxed vagina. Relax your hips and buttocks. Relax your inner thigh and your outer thigh.

# 9. Breathing and Relaxation for Labour

## Ignorance-Fear-Tension-Pain Syndrome

The uterus is made up of strong muscles whose action causes it to open and let the baby pass first through its opening (cervix), and then through the vaginal passage into the doctor's hands. Childbirth therefore depends largely on the efficient working of the muscles of the uterus and the vagina.

Muscles in our body are of 2 types, voluntary muscles and the involuntary muscles. Voluntary muscles are those over which we have direct control, the muscles of the arms and legs for instance. Involuntary muscles are those over which we have no direct control, like the muscles of our heart or uterus.

If a woman is tense during labour, her uterine muscles will also get tense and perform with great difficulty, because tension in the body is infectious; it passes from one muscle to the other. However, if she is relaxed, her uterine muscles will work unhampered, and with each contraction they will get closer to complete dilation of the cervix, so that the woman will have a shorter, less painful labour.

This is called the ignorance–fear–tension–pain syndrome. That is, ignorance of how the body functions during childbirth causes a fear of the unknown. Fear causes tension, which in turn leads to rigid abdominal muscles, more pain and longer labour. Whereas, if you eliminate ignorance by understanding the physiology of birth, you eliminate the fear of the unknown. Without fear, tension will be absent, leading to easy muscle action, so that your body functions as nature intended it to, without being hampered by tension.

## Quick Relaxation in Labour

Relax the lower abdomen, pelvic floor, hips and buttocks and your thighs, each time a contraction is over. Then go on to general relaxation.

There are certain points in the body where tension tends to accumulate. If you work at relaxing these points, you will quickly achieve relaxation.

- Relax your forehead. Stop frowning. Pinch your eyebrows and stroke your forehead.
- Relax your jaw. A relaxed jaw is a relaxed vagina.
- Separate your teeth and let your tongue be static in the middle of your mouth.
- Relax your shoulders.
- Relax your elbows. Loosen them and move them away from your body.
- Relax your hands.
- Relax your feet.

If you find it difficult to relax any of these points, have your partner massage them for you. For instance, your partner can massage your shoulders, face or feet, to help you relax. Practise this daily, so that you use it with ease during labour.

Each time a contraction is over, go into relaxation. During a contraction, the uterus is partially deprived of blood and oxygen. Relaxation after the contraction sends a plentiful supply of this life-giving fluid to the uterus. When the body is relaxed, the muscles in the body use a minimum of energy, and oxygen enriched blood reaches the uterus and the baby, ensuring a healthier and alert baby. Also, using the rest periods between contractions to your maximum advantage will not allow tension to build up and accumulate in your body, keeping you relaxed right through.

When a contraction occurs, concentrate on keeping your face relaxed. If you keep your face relaxed, automatically the rest of your body will also become relaxed. Tension anywhere in the body will show on the face.

## Breathing for Labour

Properly regulated breathing during labour will help take away the pain of labour.

Breathing has to be practised regularly before delivery, so that you can slip into breathing effortlessly when you go into labour.

## Conditioned Reflex

Reflexes are instantaneous and involuntary responses to stimuli. There are 2 types of reflexes. The inborn reflex, e.g. blinking to protect the eyes from a blow, or the conditioned reflex of feeling hunger at meal times.

As an inborn reflex, a dog will salivate if meat is put in his mouth. If, however, the introduction of meat is preceded by the ringing of a bell, and this process is repeated several times, the dog ends up salivating when just the bell is rung and no meat is given. Hence, a conditioned reflex has been established, which associates food with the sound of the bell and so determines the response of salivation.

In the same way, breathing regularly practised for labour establishes a pathway to the brain which associates breathing with labour. When labour actually sets in, the brain determines the response of breathing.

121

# Breathing Focus

Breathing during labour brings about a focus of activity in one part of the brain, from where it has a tendency to develop and spread. For instance, a pupil paying attention to what the teacher is saying is not aware of noise in the street, because the attention he is paying to the teacher's lecture localises the focus of activity in his brain, and becomes surrounded by a zone of inhibition into which all the stimuli frcm surrounding noises drain. In the same way, a toothache, which is hardly noticed when one is busy with some important activity, becomes stabbing during inactivity.

The aim of preparation for labour by learning breathing patterns is to reinforce to its maximum the inhibition of the brain, by bringing about a focus of breathing activity during labour.

The strength of inhibition brought about by your focus on breathing activity will depend on the strength of your focus on your breathing patterns. This in turn will depend on the work and practice you have put into the development of this focus. The success of your labour is therefore in your hands.

This is stressed by the French doctor, Lamaze, in the psychoprophylactic method of childbirth, based on Pavlov's experiments carried out in Russia.

According to Dr. Lamaze, in the book *Painless Childbirth*, (New York, 1972), 'a woman learns how to give birth the same way she learns how to swim or write or read—and she does so without pain.'

# Breathing Patterns

*Deep cleansing breath*  Before any kind of breathing is practised, first take a deep cleansing breath. That is, you fully fill and

122

empty your lungs.

Breathe in deeply through the nose and let it out through the mouth. Take this breath at the beginning and at the end of a breathing practice.

Breathe in deeply through the nose, and breathe out slowly through your mouth, as though you were trying to flicker the flame of a burning candle held at arm's length, with the air that you are exhaling.

*Waist-level breathing*

Practise a few times.

Now, do your quick relaxation, then practise this breathing for 30 seconds, beginning and ending with a deep cleansing breath.

The number of waist-level breaths should be between 4 and 6 in 30 seconds. If it is more than 6 you are breathing too fast. Slow down your breathing accordingly.

Place your hands at your chest, below your collarbone. In addition, you can have your partner place one hand at the bra level on your back. Now breathe in and out through your mouth up to your hands, a shallow, slow, and gentle breath.

*Chest-level breathing*

So that your mouth does not get dry, place the tip of your tongue on the roof of the mouth.

Practise a few times.

Do your quick relaxation. Practise this breathing for 30 seconds, beginning and ending with a deep cleansing breath.

Count the number of chest-level breaths practised without the deep cleaning breaths. The number should be between 10 and 12 breaths in 30 seconds. If you exceed 12 breaths, slow down your breathing.

*Jaw-level breathing, 'Out'*   The jaw-level breathing entails simply saying the word 'Out' with a stress on the 'T'. Do not worry about your breathing, it will take care of itself as you say the word.

Practise a few times.

Do your quick relaxation. Practise the breathing for 30 seconds, beginning and ending with a deep cleansing breath.

You could get between 20 and 25 breaths in 30 seconds, not counting the deep cleansing breaths. If you exceed 25 breaths slow down breathing.

Now you are ready to do a breathing practice. Let us imagine you are having a contraction which slowly builds up to a peak and then tapers away.

> **Precaution**
>
> If you ever feel dizzy while doing the breathing practices, cover your nose and mouth with your palms and blow out once. Then breathe normally.
> This will re-establish the proper balance of oxygen and carbon dioxide in your body and relieve dizziness if it is experienced.

## Breathing Practice

| Your partner says | You do | Duration |
| --- | --- | --- |
| Contraction begins | A deep cleansing breath and waist-level breathing. | 15 Secs |
| It is getting stronger | Chest-level breathing | 15 Secs |
| Still stronger | Out breathing | 15 Secs |
| It's going away | Chest-level breathing | 15 Secs |
| Further away | Waist-level breathing | 15 Secs |
| It's gone | One deep cleansing breath | |

Practise this a few times with verbal instructions.

Then, practise with pressure on the wrist. At the inner wrists the nerves are sensitive, and by exerting pressure on them, we acquaint the nerves with the message that the greater the pressure, the shallower the breathing. For instance, when you walk, you do not breathe as shallow as you do when you are running.

In labour the pressure will not be given on the wrist in this manner. When labour begins, the nerve endings on the uterus will send similar messages to the brain as contractions progress. The brain will automatically respond to greater discomfort with shallower breathing, due to the earlier practice with pressure on the wrist.

Your partner should hold your wrist, and exert pressure in accordance with the verbal instructions, during a breathing practice.

| Your partner says | And... |
| --- | --- |
| Contraction begins | exerts a firm grip on the wrist |
| It's getting stronger | exerts a little more pressure |
| Still stronger | still more pressure |
| It's going away | reduces the pressure slightly |
| Further away | returns to a firm grip on the wrist |
| It's gone | releases pressure totally |

Do 5 rounds of breathing practice daily. Remember to do your quick relaxation before you begin, and repeat the relaxation after each breathing practice. You can practise on waking in the morning or before sleeping at night.

In labour you will do whatever breathing you feel like doing. What you eventually use will depend on whether you are naturally a deep or shallow breather; whether your labour is artificially induced or a natural labour, whether you are sleepy or awake, etc.

125

# Concentration Breathing

Choose a spot above the eye level. Concentrate on it. Imagine you see there the image of someone you worship, or an image of something beautiful, like a beautiful sunset you might have seen recently, or a favourite picture.

Concentrate on the image and leave your mouth open slightly. Breathe naturally and effortlessly through your mouth.

## Concentration breathing can be used as a distraction breathing.

If you are being given an internal examination, take a deep cleansing breath and go into concentration breathing, leaving your pelvic floor muscle relaxed as when passing urine.

If you are distracted by another patient, a member of the staff, or by well-meaning relatives, go into your concentration breathing. It will remove you from your immediate environment and you will not feel disturbed. You can couple your concentration breathing with the other breathing levels, that is, as you do waist–level, chest-level and out-breathing, you can concentrate on your image at the same time.

If you are wheeled into the operation theatre and want to take your attention off the frightening equipment around you, concentration-breathing will help.

When an injection is being given, or when the drip is being fixed on your arm, do the concentration breathing.

126

## Not-Pushing Breathing

The old wives' tale which says that one must push the moment labour begins, is false. Physically pushing out the baby should be done only at birth. Before birth, both lips of the cervix have to move away from baby's head.

Just before the birth of the baby, while one lip could have moved away, the other could still be covering part of the baby's head. If you push prematurely, it could cause the baby's head to hit against the unopened lip of the cervix, causing swelling and tenderness.

You might experience a desire to bear down and push the baby out, in the middle of a contraction. It is important to immediately inform the staff how you feel, and not bear down until the staff or the doctor says that you can do so. To avoid bearing down do the following breathing:

| | |
|---|---|
| 2 shallow pants | Blow |
| 2 shallow pants | Blow |
| 2 shallow pants | Blow |

If the urge to push is very strong, you may need to blow out several times in a row. That is:

| | |
|---|---|
| 2 shallow pants | Blow. Blow. Blow. |

Occasionally, some women who have had induced labours have used this breathing during labour.

## Transition

Transition is an intense period before the birth of the baby. The cervix dilates to a total of 10 cm to permit the passing of the baby's head. During

127

transition the cervix could be about 8 cm dilated (10 cm is full dilation). That is, the dilation of the cervix is soon going to be complete and the expulsion of the baby through the vagina is going to begin. There is soon going to be a transition from the first stage of labour to the second stage. Transition can last from 10 minutes to an hour approximately. It is a sign that you are almost there.

You might just sail through the transition without feeling a thing. On the other hand, you might feel cold or hot or nauseous during this phase. This is the time you need the quiet presence of your partner.

During transition your contractions are closest together. They could come 2 minutes apart and can be sharp long ones, lasting a whole minute. The 'Out' and concentration breathing should be most suitable at this stage. After transition, the contractions again become 5 minutes apart.

Typical of this stage is a premature desire to push the baby out. If you push before the cervix is fully dilated, the cervix can become swollen and resist opening up.

Transition can also be characterised by a negative change of mood. You might suddenly feel angry or discouraged or helpless or in need of a painkiller. You might be angry with the hospital set-up or your partner. You might feel discouraged that having being in labour for hours, nothing is happening. You might feel helpless at your situation and your inability to run away from it. A combination of strong contractions and a negative mood swing might tempt you to ask for a painkiller.
This is also the time when you might be offered a painkiller. Medication at this stage is best avoided, as it can slow down the birth process and require the use of instruments at birth that is, the use of forceps, or the use of vacuum extraction.

If your partner reminds you, that this must be transition and therefore a sign that you are at the end of labour, it helps. Some women find the hand squeeze comforting at this stage, whereas others do not like being touched. The unobtrusive presence of a partner is most welcome at this stage. This is the time when a woman internalises and knows she has to make a go of it all by herself. She is one with the process her body is undergoing. It is a short and intense phase.

# Pushing

When dilation of the cervix is complete to 10 cm or 5 fingers, and the baby is being pushed out through the birth canal or vagina, the second stage of labour has begun.

At this stage, you will be taken to the delivery room. The delivery room has a special table on which you will be made to lie, with your legs apart. Your legs may be supported by stirrups. Alternatively you will be told to place your legs bent at the knees and your feet placed flat on the table.

When the doctor tells you to push, you do the breathing described below.

During practice, either lie down using 2 pillows under your head, or sit with your back supported by the wall and your legs stretched out in front of you, then take:

1 waist-level breath (inhale through the nose up to your waist and blow out through pursed lips).

A 2nd waist-level breath.

129

During the 3rd waist-level breath, after inhaling, hold your breath.

While you hold your breath, incline your chin slightly towards your chest, so that whatever pressure you apply at the time of birth, does not get concentrated in the neck, and is automatically diverted towards the pelvic floor. When you cannot hold your breath any longer, it is a sign that your body needs more oxygen, so exhale and quickly inhale and resume holding your breath. When doing so you can raise your head so that exhalation and inhalation come more easily. Once done, resume bending chin towards your chest.

Do not physically apply pressure downwards as when you are constipated. Physical application of pressure is to be practiced only at the time of actual birth. When practicing, just practise holding your breath, and then release your pelvic floor as when passing urine.

So when you feel the start of a contraction and are told to push, you do:

Waist-level,
Waist-level,
Waist-level. Hold it. (Incline chin towards chest, and relax the pelvic floor.)

Exhale, inhale (if needed).
Hold it.
Do your quick relaxation when the contraction is gone.

# 10. Induced Labour

## The Estimated Date of Delivery

The estimated date of delivery is not a date of appointment. It is simply a date arrived at by a rough calculation, to estimate the average duration of pregnancy. A pregnancy might exceed it or terminate before it. Studies show that only 4 to 5% of babies arrive on the estimated date of delivery.

On an average a pregnancy lasts 280 days, 40 weeks, or 9 months and 7 days, after the first day of the last menstrual period. There is no disadvantage to the baby if the birth takes place any time between 38 and 42 weeks of pregnancy.

To calculate a woman's estimated date of delivery, one takes into account the last menstrual period before her pregnancy. Suppose it began on 25 March, one would count 7 days ahead and arrive at 1 April. Then one would count backwards 3 months, that is 1, March, 1 February, 1 January. The estimated date of delivery would be 1 January. This is a short-cut to counting 280 days from a fixed date.

However 40 weeks or 280 days is merely an average. The maturity of the baby could be anywhere from the 38th week to the 42nd week.

The actual birth date of the baby will be influenced by the menstrual cycle of the mother. Some women have a 25 or a 28 day menstrual cycle, while others may have a 35 or 40 day menstrual cycle. Ovulation and conception generally occurs about 14 days before the onset of the next period. A woman with a 25 day cycle will have conceived sooner and will deliver sooner than a woman with a 35 day cycle, since the gap between her periods is shorter than the gap of a woman who has a 35 day cycle. A lengthy cycle would mean birth beyond the due date. In calculating the estimated date of delivery it is important for a woman to be sure of her dates.

A woman with a regular cycle will deliver more predictably than one with an irregular cycle. A twin pregnancy could be shorter by 3 weeks. Triplet and quadruplet pregnancies could be shorter still. However, it is better to retain the pregnancy until full term, so it is important to avoid physical stress in the last few weeks of a multiple pregnancy. It is better for the babies.

A woman who has been on the pill may conceive without having regular periods. It is a good idea to use some other contraceptive after the pill has been stopped and have at least 3 regular periods before conception.

Although the exact reason why labour starts when it does is not known, there is a great amount of evidence that shows that the fetus, when it is ready for existing outside the womb, produces a hormone which leads to the onset of labour.

## When Labour is Induced

Induction is a way of artificially stimulating the uterus into labour contractions, with the intention of controlling the birth of the baby.

Sometimes labour may be induced for the sake of your convenience or the doctor's. Your convenience could be your desire to rejoin work on a particular date, to time a transfer of residence to your convenience, or to attend a wedding or some social function. The doctor's convenience may be a plan to attend a long-awaited medical meeting or a long-planned vacation. Or it could be the timing of the birth at a time when most medical staff are on duty.

For an induction to be successful, the baby must be full term and term size, with its head pressing down at the mouth of the womb, which should be soft, short and partially dilated. If these conditions are absent, the induction can terminate in a Caesarean section.

As you go past your due date you might begin to get anxious about when the birth will take place. People who phone and ask what news there is, only add to your anxiety. The doctor may have told you that if you go past your due date labour may be induced.

Doctors are divided in their opinion as to when labour should be induced for post-maturity. When everything is normal, some doctors would not mind allowing a pregnancy up to 43 weeks. Each pregnancy should be treated as an individual case. Certain factors like hypertension or toxaemia would warrant an induction.

## Different Methods of Induction

Earlier at full term women used to be given castor oil, and the next day labour would be triggered off if they were really ready to go into labour. Sometimes it was coupled with a hot bath and enema.

*Castor-oil*

About 25 to 50 ml of castor oil could be whisked in a hot sweetened cup of milk and drunk by the woman a night before she is scheduled for an induction of labour.

| | |
|---|---|
| *Sweeping and Stretching or stripping* | Just before or during labour, when the cervix is lax, this procedure can be carried out. About 25 to 50 ml of castor oil could be whisked in a hot sweetened cup of milk and drunk by the woman a night before she is scheduled for an induction of labour. While an internal vaginal examination is being given, the membranes of the water bag are swept off the wall of the uterus around its mouth, by the fingers, and the cervix is also stretched a little by the fingers. This speeds up labour. It may be followed by an induction. |
| *Gel or Pessary* | A gel or pessary containing prostaglandin hormone could be placed at the mouth of the womb or cervix during a vaginal examination. As it melts and comes in contact with the cervix, it causes it to soften in preparation for birth. |
| *Artificial Rupture of Membranes* | Artificial rupture of membranes, often referred to as ARM, consists of artificially rupturing the membrane of the bag of waters surrounding the baby in the womb. It is done during an internal vaginal examination. |

If the membranes are not made to rupture, they might rupture spontaneously during the course of labour, more typically when dilation of the cervix has been completed. In some instances the membranes may rupture at birth.

After the bag is made to burst, the contractions will increase in intensity. ARM speeds up labour, and is one way of inducing contractions. It is useful in prolonged labours with little progress. It is also useful when the fetal heart shows signs of distress. The breaking of the water then facilitates the doctor to check the water for meconium staining. If the water is coloured green or muddy coloured from the baby's stool, it is a sign of distress, for the baby normally should pass the first stool after birth, not in the uterus.

Dr. Ian Donald says in his *Practical Obstetric Problems:* 'With very few exceptions, intact membranes mean an intact mother and an intact baby.'

There are also fewer chances of cord prolapse when the membranes are intact. Cord prolapse occurs when the cord on being swept down with the waters, comes to lie between the bones of the pelvis and the baby's head, causing distress to the baby. Pressure on the cord is another possibility when the rupture of membranes causes powerful contractions that exert pressure on the cord and reduce the flow of blood and oxygen to the baby.

When the membranes are intact there are fewer chances of infection. Also, intact membranes mean that an even hydrostatic pressure is applied to the whole fetal surface, so that the birth experience is gentler for the baby.

When a baby is born with membranes intact, there is less likelihood of the uterus closing up after the birth of the baby, and before the delivery of the placenta.

Keeping all these points in mind, routine ARM is most undesirable.

---

An injection of pitocin may be given in the arm or on the hip. Pitocin speeds up labour when contractions become lax. Once labour is established a course of 3 to 5 apidocin injections may be given to speed up the opening up or dilation of the cervix.    *Intramuscular injection*

---

The commonly used procedure for induction these days is to trigger off labour with the use of synthetic form of the oxytocin hormone, which in natural labour is    *Intravenous drip*

135

secreted by the mother's pituitary gland and makes the uterus contract. The artificial form of oxytocin, called syntocin, is added to a bottle of glucose solution and introduced straight into the mother's blood stream through a drip attached to her arm. A fine needle is inserted into a vein in the arm and kept in place.

Doctors like to use the drip because the glucose gives you energy without your needing to eat anything. So if a Caesarean section is needed, your stomach is likely to be empty as needed for the administration of anaesthesia. If you eat, there is the risk that while under anaesthesia you might vomit and inhale the contents of it. Glucose or dextrose solution drips energy straight into your veins, bypassing the stomach.

The energy you can get from glucose will be useful if you have had a long-drawn labour and become tired. So while in labour you can also drink glucose dissolved in water, with the consent of your doctor, when you begin to feel tired.

Once a drip is set up, any drug apart from syntocin can be introduced into the blood stream through it, without your being aware of it. If you are on the drip, each time the bottle is changed ask what it is. The bottle would have 'Synto' written on it to indicate the syntocin hormone.

Routine use of the drip is best avoided. It will make you immobile in labour, confining you to the bed. It will also make labour sharper and stronger, unnecessarily adding to your discomfort. There are times, such as prolonged labour, when a drip may be needed.

Labour may be triggered off by the intravenous glucose drip in certain conditions like toxaemia, very

136

high blood pressure, diabetes, prolonged pregnancy, if some hours have elapsed after the bag has burst and labour has not begun on its own.

If you happen to need the drip, remember to pass urine frequently while on it, to avoid your bladder getting very full. Request for the glucose bottle to be fixed on a stand with wheels, rather than for it to be fixed to the side of your bed. That would allow you to go to the toilet when required and also allow general mobility. If the drip is fixed to the side of your bed, request for a long tube so that you can turn over and move about in bed. If it is short, you will feel trapped. Avoid putting weight on the arm on which the drip is fixed.

# Home Inductions

If your partner sucks at your nipples, or either of you stroke and massage the nipples and the breasts, it will stimulate the release of oxytocin hormones in your body, and if your body is ready, over a period of time, it can cause labour to start. Applying a warm cloth to your breasts can have the same effect. 15 days before your estimated date of delivery, you can take a mug of warm water and dip two face towels in it. Wring the water out of them and apply them on the front of the breast, so that they cover the nipple, and areola. This will cause you to feel a pleasant warm sensation. When you feel this, remove the towels and dip them in water again and re-apply them on the breast. Do 6 times altogether. Repeat 4 times a day. Morning, afternoon, evening and night.

*Breast stimulation*

At the Letterman Army Medical Center in San Francisco, 2 groups of a 100 women each in the 39th week of pregnancy were instructed to rub both nipples gently between their fingertips for an hour, thrice daily. By the 42nd week 89 breast stimulators had gone into spontaneous labour, as compared with 77 non–breast stimulators in the other groups. Also only 5 breast stimulators had unripe cervixes as compared to 17 in the other group *(see p.103).*

*Intercourse*

If your delivery is overdue and the doctor says an induction may be considered, it is a good idea to indulge in intercourse. Seminal fluid is rich in prostoglandin hormones which are known to ripen the cervix and stimulate contractions. The cervix is thus affected locally and labour begins more naturally as compared to being put on the intravenous drip in the hospital *(see p.102).*

The growth of the baby is estimated not by the largeness of the mother's abdomen but by the height of the growing uterus. It is only in about the 4th month that the pregnancy begins to show externally, as the abdomen enlarges. A few weeks before delivery the uterus may drop or lower as the baby's head goes into the pelvis.

## Prolonged Pregnancy

A pregnancy can go 14 days over the estimated date of delivery. However, most obstetricians do not like the pregnancy to prolong beyond 7 to 10 days after the estimated date of delivery. If pregnancy goes more than 14 days beyond the due date, doctors are concerned that:

9 MONTHS
BEFORE DELIVERY
6 MONTHS

3 MONTHS

■ Beyond this time the placenta begins to get fibrous and its efficiency to nourish the baby decreases.

■ The measure of amniotic fluid dwindles as the baby gets bigger, so it could result in a dry labour.

138

- The cranial or head bones harden and no moulding of the head takes place during birth.

Whether labour needs to be induced or not depends on the baby's well–being. The baby's well-being can be assessed in the following ways:

---

If the fetal heart rate is normal, it is a sign that all is well with the baby. The average fetal heart rate is 140 beats per minute. It could vary slightly. Your doctor would know what the heartbeat of your baby has been throughout pregnancy.

*Fetal heart rate*

---

Placental insufficiency will be suspected if the doctor feels that the baby is not growing, since the size of the uterus will be smaller than it should be. This could occur in underweight, malnourished women, in women prone to drug abuse, women with high blood pressure, chronic kidney disease or diabetes. It could also happen in women prone to pre–eclampsia, heart, lung or gastro–intestinal disorders, and women suffering from infection.

*Placental insufficiency I.U.G.R.*

According to the book *Obstetrics and the Newborn*, 1997, in case of I.U.G.R., the second baby is likely to fare much better than the first baby.

If the doctor suspects a slow fetal growth, improve your diet. If you are already eating well, rest. Rest encourages blood flow to the uterus and the baby, and after bed rest, a sudden spurt in the baby's growth may be noticed at the next checkup. As you rest, favour lying on your side to lying on your back, it will encourage greater blood and oxygen supply to the baby. Lying on the left side encourages optimum oxygen supply to the baby. Avoid a smoke–filled atmosphere.

If this does not help the baby's growth, the baby may be delivered by a Caesarean section or labour may be induced, depending on what the doctor thinks best.

*Diabetic mother*

Some women may develop diabetes in pregnancy, while some others may be diabetic to begin with.

Diabetes that starts in pregnancy is called gestational diabetes, and is more likely to occur in the last 3 months of pregnancy. A high glucose level in early pregnancy could mean that the mother was diabetic before pregnancy without realising it. Most women who develop gestational diabetes will find that their glucose levels return to normal after delivery. However, gestational diabetes could return with the next pregnancy. The possibility can be reduced by following a healthy diet and not putting on too much weight.

Frequently, pregnant women may show glucose in their urine without having diabetes, as, in pregnancy the resistance level at which glucose spills into the urine comes down. A glucose tolerance test can identify whether the woman has an unusually low renal threshold, but not diabetes, or whether she has diabetes.

Women who are diabetic before becoming pregnant have an excess of blood sugar which the baby absorbs and tends to become very large. The doctor will recommend a restriction of sweet foods to these mothers.

A diabetic mother may be induced early so that the baby does not get so big that a safe vaginal delivery is impossible. Despite its large size, the baby may not be mature and may need special care after birth. Sometimes if the cervix is not soft and ready to open up, a Caesarean section may be performed.

Whether you develop diabetes will depend on whether there is a history of diabetes in your family. Also women who have previously given birth to exceptionally large babies, say 4 kilograms or 9 pounds, may be prone to diabetes. Often diabetes disappears after the birth of the baby. However, it is a sign that you have latent diabetes and it would be a good idea to keep a check on your diet and weight.

| | |
|---|---|
| When a woman's blood pressure is up the whole day (not only when she visits the clinic), when she has albumin in the urine and when she is retaining fluids so that her fingers, ankles and possibly her face is swollen, she would have toxaemia. A woman with toxaemia might also have a sudden weight gain. In severe toxaemia—the placenta, which nourishes the baby—provides it with oxygen and helps excrete its waste products, will not be able to function well, so that there is a risk to the baby. In such cases, labour will be induced so that the baby is born while the placenta is still functioning well (*see p.57*). | *Toxaemia* |

| | |
|---|---|
| In the last 3 months of pregnancy, when a woman's blood pressure is checked during an antenatal visit and it is found to be high, say 140/90 or more, the doctor will try and treat the high blood pressure so that the pregnancy can be maintained to allow adequate growth and maturity of the fetus, so that it will be able to survive at birth. Often rest might control the blood pressure. If required, sedation may be given to control it. If these measures are inadequate, labour may be induced (*see p.57*). | *Very high blood pressure* |

| | |
|---|---|
| *When the water bag bursts* | When the water bag bursts in a great gush, and contractions do not start spontaneously, an induction is set up to deliver the baby within 24 hours, beyond 24 hours the risk of infection sets in. Interestingly the risk of infection rises with each internal examination. |
| | There is no harm if you wait for 4 to 5 hours or longer after the bursting of the bag before the drip is fixed. It is possible that as you wait, the contractions may start on their own. Contractions that start spontaneously are gentler and less intense than those induced by drip. |
| *Prolonged labour* | When labour lasts for many hours without progress, say approximately 12 to 18 hours, an induction could speed up the progress of labour. |
| *Rhesus negative* | If you are rhesus–negative and there is a possibility that your baby is going to need blood transfusion at birth, labour may be induced so that your baby will be born at a time when laboratory facilities, the paediatrician and other staff will be available. This will be the case if, while you are pregnant, you have a positive antibody test, that is, a blood test reveals that you have antibodies in your system *(see p.60)*. However, this danger today is almost non existent, since an injection of anti-D immunoglobin is given to the mother in the ante-natal period as a preventive. |

# 11. Birth

Straightforward uncomplicated birth comprises 3 distinct stages. In the 1st stage of labour the mouth of the womb opens up and dilates to make way for the baby's head to pass through. In the 2nd stage of labour the baby passes through the vagina and is born. In the 3rd stage of labour, the placenta is delivered, having completed its function of nourishing the baby.

---

The 1st stage is the longest – about 12 hours with a little plus or minus. The 2nd stage could be from 30 minutes to an hour and a half and the 3rd stage could take about 10 minutes. In the first delivery, the 1st stage is usually longer than in subsequent births.

*The first stage of labour*

In the 1st stage, the lips of the womb or cervix thin out and stretch apart over the baby's head, while the body of the uterus shrinks on the baby and pushes it towards the cervix. This is what happens during the contraction or pain of labour. Sometimes before contractions are felt, a harmless, thick mucus discharge may be noticed. On the other hand, a water leak may herald the onset of labour *(see p.107)*.

When you go to the hospital, your husband or relative will be given certain forms to be filled up, while you will be taken to a room where you will be told to change into a hospital gown. Then your pubic hair will be shaved. It will be followed by an enema. An enema is a process whereby a tube is inserted in the anus and a fluid flushes the bowels thoroughly. This avoids the passing of stool during birth. Often after an enema, contractions become stronger. Remember, an empty rectum and an empty bladder will aid the progress of labour, so in labour pass stool whenever you desire to and keep drinking fluids

143

and pass urine every 60 to 90 minutes. A full bladder can cause discomfort and pain and inhibit uterine contractions. Later it can lead to diminished bladder tone and infection. Do not limit your fluid intake. You will specially get thirsty if you perspire a lot.

After the enema, your husband or relative will be permitted to join you, and can be with you until when you are ready for birth, and taken into the delivery room. If you have booked in a big hospital, you may not be permitted to have your husband or relative with you.

During labour your blood pressure could be taken now and then. The nurse would also take your pulse and temperature, and listen to the baby's heartbeat. The position of the baby may be ascertained by palpitating your abdomen or by an internal examination. An internal examination could also be carried out to check how many centimetres the cervix has dilated. A note would be made of whether the membranes have ruptured and whether there is any bleeding, you will be asked when and what you ate last and whether you have taken any medication.

Labour can begin quite gently and build up to powerful sensations. Between contractions, you must make an effort to practise quick relaxation. If labour starts during the day, move about the house at leisure. If labour starts in the evening or night, try and get some sleep. Do not tire yourself out by being physically overactive. Conserve your energy for the other half of labour, but do try and remain upright. When you are upright, the pressure of the baby's head on the cervix will stimulate your uterus to contract. If you lie down for a while, remember lying on your side is better than lying on your back, since it relieves pressure on the vena cava, a major blood vessel, so that the oxygen content of your blood is enhanced, much to your and the baby's advantage.

You will find further details on how you can remain upright and when not to remain upright in the chapter *Labour Time*.

Labour can be handled quite comfortably with breathing, various positions and relaxation techniques. However, there are some drugs that are used for pain relief in labour. Their use will depend on the discretion of your obstetrician. You may or may not need them during labour.

Drugs, analgesics and anesthetics are sometimes administered, although they are often unnecessary and can have harmful side effects. Refrain from asking for them. Family members accompanying the woman in labour should avoid becoming unnecessarily anxious, constantly requesting the doctor to do something. Labour will take its own time.

Some women may have an unnatural or difficult birth. Complications sometimes occur, in which case you must leave the decisions to your doctor. Some complications could arise in labour, whereas in some cases risk factors are already present, for instance, a woman with a previous Caesarean delivery, a previous stillbirth, kidney problems, or diabetes. In such cases a good public hospital, if situated within reachable distance, is a good choice. A big public hospital would have a highly experienced and qualified staff, blood bank facilities, a paediatric unit to take care of the newborn and there would be no commercial pressures.

The 2nd stage of labour is recognised by strong contractions coming every 1 to 2 minutes and lasting a whole minute. After a while the contractions will slow

*Second stage of labour*

# Prepared Childbirth

If labour progresses without drugs, while a woman uses prepared childbirth techniques or naturally handles labour in a relaxed way, the body produces endorphin hormones. Endorphins are natural painkillers and are secreted by the body during hard physical exercise and labour.

Some prepared childbirth methods concentrate only on psychologically training a woman for birth, while other methods equip a woman to deal with labour by using certain breathing rhythms, as explained in this book, in the chapter *Breathing and Relaxation for Labour*.

Prepared childbirth is ideal for a woman who would prefer to avoid medication in labour either completely or as long as possible. Just moving about in labour from one position to another, as one desires, reduces the discomfort of labour greatly. So does the practice of breathing and relaxation.

Painkillers are often freely offered and accepted in labour because in our civilised society nobody likes to lose emotional control. As women often say, 'I don't want to make an ass of myself'; It is not socially acceptable for a woman to make a show of her feelings in labour. She is expected to be a patient who lies down quietly in her bed making as little noise as possible. Women often do not realise that they have another option.

It is best to avoid any kind of drug in labour, since whatever you inhale or receive intramuscularly, or through the drip while in labour, passes to the baby through the placenta in a matter of minutes. What you receive will be given to you in accordance with your body weight and it immediately passes to the baby who is only a fraction of your weight. So a drug that will make you sleepy or knock you out, will do the same, manifold, to the baby.

Most sedatives and painkillers given to

the mother would depress her breathing and lower her blood pressure, doing the same to the baby. As a result the baby would be born sluggish, which may jeopardise the baby's respiration in the few precious moments after birth. Lack of oxygen at birth can have a serious effect on the child's brain, even if mild; it can affect its ability to learn in later years.

Drugs must be used with great caution if the baby is premature or small, because the baby's liver will be immature and will find it difficult to break down the drugs and eliminate them from the body. In labour, a drug, in order to be of use, should not be given in so large a dose that it results in dangerous side effects. At the same time the dose should be large enough to give the desired effects, that is, the dose should not be too small and therefore ineffective.

The more medication a mother receives in labour, the longer and more difficult will be the baby's adjustment to life after birth. Medication can also affect breastfeeding negatively, especially in the first 5 days.

Most mammals like to have their babies in a quiet dark corner, where, left to themselves, they move about restlessly and deliver by themselves. People having pets may have noticed this kind of behaviour in dogs and cats. Human beings with their learned behaviour find it difficult to regress to such natural primitive behaviour.

A woman should learn to flow with her body and experience the birth of her baby as a basic function of her body. Each contraction should be considered an effort of her body to give birth to her baby. Handled positively and naturally, many women speak of the delight of feeling the baby's body slip through, of feeling a warmness and a wetness followed by the baby's cry. Whereas many drugged or anaesthetised women may feel they missed out on it all.

Two obstetricians, Dr. Dick Read and Dr. Lamaze, taught women how to cope with labour. Dr. Read stressed relaxation and understanding labour in order to remove fear. Dr. Lamaze stressed teaching preconditioned breathing responses to women to use at the time of labour. Presently, Dr. Michel Odent is teaching women how to regress to primitive consciousness in labour, by being given quiet and gentle support by birth attendants, while the labouring woman moves instinctively to find naturally comfortable positions. She is encouraged to forget what her culture has told her about labour, and to be in touch with her body.

down. Typical of this stage is also the desire on your part to bear down and push the baby out. Some women feel nauseous at this stage of labour. The 2nd stage of labour begins when the cervix has dilated to its full 10 cm and ends with the delivery of the baby. At this stage you are taken into the delivery room and made to lie down on your back with legs bent at the knees and feet resting flat on the bed. Alternatively, you will be made to lie down on your back and your legs will be supported by a set of stirrups on either side of the delivery table, so that your legs after being bent at the knee would be supported wide apart on either side. The stirrup would support the back of your bent knee and ankles.

This is often referred to as the working stage of labour, for you have to work along with the uterine contractions to expel the baby and deliver it, by adding your efforts to physically push the baby out.

At this stage the folds in the vagina unfold to accommodate the baby's head. The pressure of the baby's head on the pelvic floor gives a feeling of fullness in the rectum, which many women describe as a desire to pass stool. Finally the baby's head comes in contact with the perineum or the muscular outlet of the pelvis, which is stretched until the baby's head appears through it, just as your head would appear out of the top of a polo neck sweater when you are putting it on. The baby's head is normally delivered face down and the back of the head towards the ceiling. After the head is delivered, the baby's shoulders appear, followed quickly by the rest of its body. You may hear your baby's cry or whimper. The absence of loud cry does not mean that something is wrong.

*Third stage of labour*

This stage begins with the birth of the baby and ends with the expulsion of the placenta, which peels away from the wall of the uterus and is delivered after the baby.

After the birth of the baby, the umbilical cord continues to pulsate and supply the baby with oxygen through the placenta, while simultaneously, the baby's own breathing gets established. The cord is clamped a few inches away from the baby's navel and a few inches away it is incised between the two clamps. A stump of the cord will be left on the baby's abdomen. After a few days the stump will dry up and fall off, leaving the baby's navel as a permanent mark of its past existence.

The baby is born with mucus or fluid in its nose, mouth and throat. Some of it is wiped away when the head is delivered. After birth the baby is kept head down to encourage further draining of the mucus. If the mucus seems to be interfering with the baby's first breath and there are chances of it being inhaled, it will be removed by a suction device. A little mucus remaining in the baby's lungs gets absorbed into the bloodstream when the baby's breathing is well established. At birth the baby's lungs are in a collapsed state like deflated balloons, stickily held together by mucus. The first breath fills them with air. The filling of the lungs with air causes blood to rush to them and the oxygen from the air is absorbed by the baby's bloodstream. When this happens the baby's blood circulation switches from receiving oxygen from the placenta to receiving oxygen from the baby's lungs.

The baby's heart starts to function. The artery that fed the baby's heart blood from the placenta stops functioning when the cord is incised, and the baby's heart begins to function independently.

The delivery of the placenta is not unpleasant or painful. The last few contractions cause the placenta to detach from the wall of the uterus and it is delivered through the birth canal. Sometimes an injection of syntometrine or syntocinon is given to make the uterus contract and hasten this stage. Sometimes the doctor tugs at the cord and at the same time the abdomen may be massaged to help free the placenta from the uterus. On the other hand, after 10 to 15 minutes of the birth, uterine contractions spontaneously start again. They take another 10 to 15 minutes to become strong enough to separate the placenta from the uterine wall and expel it.

The doctor checks the placenta to see that it has come out whole. Bits of it left inside can create problems later, of heavy bleeding and passing of clots.

## The Baby at Birth

At birth a baby looks wet with plastered down hair. The body is covered with a cheesy substance called vernix which gives waterproof protection to the baby in the uterus. The baby might also be streaked with a little blood. At first the baby may look blue, but will change to a pink shade as its circulation gets established. At first the baby breathes around 110 breaths per minute and may cough and splutter or gasp.

Occasionally the baby's head might be a little oddly shaped as a result of its moulding during birth. The baby's breast may also be enlarged in either sex. A male baby's testes may seem blue and enlarged. A female baby's labia may be red and swollen. The baby may be covered with fine hair. After a few days the oddities of appearance will disappear.

# 12. Gentle Birth

In recent years the limelight has shifted from the labouring mother to the labouring baby. At first all attention was focused on providing pain relief to the mother. Now, science has realised that the baby is not born deaf and insensitive to its environment as was previously believed. The baby is very sensitive to light, sound and touch. Just as the mother labours to give birth, the baby labours to be born, to wriggle itself out of the birth passage, to see the light of day.

Birth is also painful for the baby. How painful, one cannot say, since no one remembers the birth experience. Until labour begins, the baby is safe inside the warm waters in the uterus. The baby does not have to breathe. Its body is supplied with oxygen through the umbilical cord. It is never hungry or thirsty. Nourishment reaches the baby through the cord. It is nurtured by the placenta and the umbilical cord and feels safe and familiar with its environment. Suddenly, the nurturing womb becomes hostile and begins to shrink on it, the space getting more cramped with each contraction. It gets expelled towards the opening in the mouth of the womb. From the womb it is propelled further down towards the birth passage. Realising the inevitable expulsive efforts of the womb, the baby also tries to struggle free in the direction of the expulsive forces. It joins in the struggle in the hope of setting itself free of these incomprehensible forces.

Finally comes freedom, or birth. And what does the baby encounter? In order to survive, it has to breathe, and quickly. For the cord supplying it with oxygen is cut immediately. Its lungs fill with air for the first time in its life, and it probably feels the passage of air searing in, and finally reach in its lungs to inflate them instantaneously like bicycle tyres. There is blinding light, which causes it to close its eyes. It gets held upside down and probably slapped, so that its cry can reassure birth attendants that it is well.

There are strange sounds or deafening noises. Its skin, used to the soft touch of warm water, experiences the rough feel of fabric. It gets laid on a cold, hard table. Tubes may be pushed into its nose or mouth right down to its lungs. Burning eye drops may be put in its eyes.

In other words, the trauma of labour is followed by the trauma of birth. Today, many psychologists feel that the trauma of birth can leave a permanent mark on the baby's psychology. Also many obstetricians believe that the trauma of birth can be greatly reduced by giving a warmer welcome to the baby at birth.

## D R . R . D . L A I N G

According to him when the baby is born, the umbilical cord is wet and pulsating. It is full of blood which reaches the baby through it, from the placenta. As soon as the baby is born, the doctor clamps the cord and cuts it. It takes approximately 5 minutes for the baby's own blood circulation to establish. If the cord is not cut immediately, it gives the baby oxygen while this transition is being made. The blood vessels carrying blood from the cord seal off as the baby's own system of circulation takes over. So if the cord is cut after the newborn's own circulation has taken over, the newborn's adjustment to breathing and the world will be smoother and gentler.

## D R . F R E D E R I C K L E B O Y E R

Dr. Leboyer, a French obstetrician, feels that the baby's cry at birth is a cry of anguish from the pain it suffers. He believes the baby should be delivered in a gentle and loving environment of dim lights and hushed voices. The newborn baby should be lifted and placed face down on the mother's abdomen. The mother should gently massage the baby's back as it unfolds into the world. The cord should be cut after it has stopped pulsating, even though the baby would have been breathing on its own for some time.

Leboyer in his book, *Birth without Violence* ( U.K., 1975 ), says, 'Instead of howling as expected, each baby merely uttered two or three healthy cries and then contented itself with powerful breathing. So that in the silence that followed, what each woman heard was the very absence of her baby's cry. Her eyes soon betrayed first surprise and then alarm, darting questioningly from one of us to the next.'

'Why isn't my baby crying ?' They seemed positively aggrieved. The surprise, the regret, the accusation in those questions dumbfounded us. We had not realised how deeply ingrained is the assumption that the newborn child must cry, how profound is the unconscious acceptance that birth and suffering are one.

'To be fair, we must admit that a newborn baby who begins gurgling happily after just a cry or two, who yawns and stretches, who enters life the way we awake from a restful sleep — is something of a surprise.

'When a child comes into the world, it must undoubtedly cry. But it need not weep.'

Once the cord is cut, Dr. Leboyer believes the baby should be lowered gently in a small tub or basin of warm water. The baby will feel the warm lightness of moving in water, just as when it was safe and warm in the water bag, in the mother's womb.

## DR. MICHEL ODENT

Dr. Odent has been greatly influenced by Dr. Leboyer's teachings.

However, while Dr. Leboyer concentrates on the baby, Dr. Odent also takes into account the woman in labour. He believes that a woman should be trained to accept labour as a very natural process of her body, and that she should regress to her primitive consciousness to be in touch with her body while it is accomplishing a very basic function. Women should be taught various upright positions they can adopt in labour. In labour a woman should do whatever she wants to. She can go through labour as she likes.

If she wants to scream, she screams. If she wants to sit she sits, walks if she wants. The room where she delivers has no menacing stainless steel equipment exposed. It is done up in warm shades of orange and brown. The room is softly lit and comfortable. It could have a low platform, cushions and birthing chair. A woman is told to remain upright in labour and to give birth in squatting position, just as advocated by the traditional Indian *dais* (midwives).

Dr. Odent feels this is specially useful in delivering breech babies, or babies being born feet first. When a mother is squatting at birth, a breech baby gets born much faster, so that the danger of the baby breathing in mucus before the head is delivered is greatly reduced.

Dr. Odent also has a small pool of warm water in which a woman in labour can sit. The warm water relaxes a woman's tense muscles and eases contractions. Babies are sometimes born in the pool of warm water when the mother does not desire to leave the pool. The baby emerges into the water while it is still getting oxygen from the umbilical cord. It transfers from the watery medium of the womb to the watery medium of the pool. It breathes when it is lifted out of the water of the pool.

Dr. Odent's uniqueness lies in his belief that each woman possesses an instinctive ability to give birth naturally. This ability is held suspect by modern obstetric practice which concentrate on skills to control labour. Dr. Odent witnesses each birth as it occurs and does not intervene in any way. He does not use pain–killing drugs, synthetic hormones, epidurals or forceps. He believes that without any medical intervention the body releases complex neurohormones. It is on the natural balance of these hormones that spontaneous labour depends.

Dr. Odent in his book, *Birth Reborn* ( U.K., 1986), says, 'It has also become more and more obvious that endorphins play an important role in the complex hormonal equilibrium that makes a spontaneous delivery possible. Neurohormones with morphine like functions, these 'endogenous opiates', act as natural pain–killers, not only protecting against pain but also suppressing anxiety and inducing a general feeling of wellbeing. High levels of endorphins may, for example, induce so called alpha brain waves that are associated with states of serenity or beatitude. It is almost as if people have always sensed the presence of this natural capacity for wellbeing and sought ways to trigger it. Running, for example, raises our endorphin levels; prayer, meditation, yoga and acupuncture may do the same.'

After the baby is born, it is placed on its stomach, on a soft towel between the mother's legs. The baby's head is turned to a side so that if the baby has some liquid in the mouth, gravity helps to drain it out and prevent it from entering the baby's lungs. The baby lies like this until it lets out a cry and takes some deep breaths, coughs, sneezes and shows good body tone. The room is heated to a comfortable temperature or the baby is covered with a blanket. Then the baby is scooped up by the mother in her arms while it is still linked to her body by the cord. In the first half hour or so after birth, mother and baby get to know each other. The cord is cut unhurriedly after this first contact has been made.

Although Dr. Leboyer and Dr. Odent strongly believe in gentle birth, they are backed up by a full medical team should emergencies occur. They know how to look out for maternal or fetal distress, should it occur, and how to take care of it. Dr. Leboyer points out that mother and child should never be allowed to go short on oxygen. Dr. Odent performs Caesarean sections when they are necessary. Interestingly, their Caesarean section rate and their rate of babies dying are lower than the average.

| Caesarean Section Rates | |
| --- | --- |
| Dr. Odent | 6 to 7% |
| U.S.A. | 19% |
| U.K. | 13% |
| France | 15% |

*(Source :* Birth Reborn *by Dr. M. Odent p. 101)*

In France perinatal mortality rates (i.e. death immediately before or after birth) rates in the last 8 years have dropped from 20 per 1,000 to 10 per 1,000. Dr. Leboyer is said to have greatly contributed to this.

# 13. After Childbirth

Immediately after the birth of the baby you may not be overcome by a gush of maternal love and instincts. You might even be a little disappointed by the way your baby looks. This is quite normal. As you begin to breastfeed and care for your baby, as you see your baby respond to you, your maternal feelings will be aroused and a deep love for your baby will bloom.

It is a good idea to take a laxative tablet like Dulcolax after the birth of the baby, so that you can pass the first stool with ease. Other tablets that may be prescribed by your doctor could be Calmpose to make you sleep and antibiotics for your stitches, pain-killers, or tablets for bleeding.

After the birth of the baby, and always afterwards, do not wash yourself from the anus towards the vagina after passing a stool. You could infect your stitches and make them septic or cause yourself a urinary tract infection. Wash the anal area separately with soap, after passing a stool.

## After a Normal Birth

After a normal vaginal delivery of the baby, you may find that you have to contend with discomfort in some parts of your body. Your breasts for instance, a few days after birth, would become full/swollen/sensitive as the milk comes in. Pressing out some milk when this happens will help relieve the discomfort. Sometimes you might experience mild contractions while feeding, for, as you feed, hormones are released that contract the uterus and encourage it to involute close to its pre-pregnant size. Practise waist-level breathing to get over this discomfort.

Your perineum or pelvic floor may be sore from the stitches, so for the first 4 to 5 days sitting may be a problem. It will help if you use a round rubber tube to sit upon, like the one children use in swimming pools. It will avoid direct pressure on the perineum when you are sitting, so healing will be quick and the discomfort less; specially when you sit up to breastfeed the baby. If during your bath you bathe the perineum and the whole vaginal area with a mug of warm water to which a few drops, 8 or 10, of the homoeopathic medicine Calendula Q have been added, the healing will be much faster. The doctor will give you an ointment to apply, a mycin, and perhaps an anesthetic ointment.

> ### Precaution
> If you bend forward when passing urine you prevent it dribbling backwards towards the vagina/vaginal stitches. This prevents infections.

Your stomach will feel jelly-like, loose and unstable. You must exercise your abdominal muscles in the first few weeks to regain abdominal tone. *(See postnatal exercises below.)*

Avoid wearing a corset or binding cloth around your abdomen. It will only get your muscles used to artificial support. The minute the support is removed, the muscles will sag.

Changing baby's diaper

Immediately after birth the muscles are still under the influence of relaxing hormones. The exercises you do should merely coax the muscles back to their original position from their stretched positions. Special exercises are needed for this. Avoid squatting exercises. Do not lift both legs together when lying on your back. It will cause great strain in the lower back. Do not cycle in the air.

Since your muscles are in a relaxed state and your body, especially your back, has been overstrained, get extra help to take care of household chores for this period so that you can rest and take it easy.

**Tackling household chores**

When you work, say, when you wash or iron, make sure that you do so without unnecessary exertion. That is, sit comfortably on a low stool when you wash the diapers. Make sure the ironing surface is the correct height for you. You should not have to bend when you iron or push the baby's pram or cook. Keep your elbows relaxed and do not tense your shoulders. Overstrain, when performing simple day–to–day tasks, can give rise to discomfort or pain in some of the muscles in your body. If you are unlucky, this pain might stay with you even later; so make sure you do not overstrain. Do not lift anything heavy. When lifting anything of moderate weight, bend knees and keep the back straight as you do so. Whenever you bend down to make the bed or pick up something you may have dropped, pull in your abdomen first.

Your lower abdomen may be streaked with brown or purple lines. These lines will slowly fade to white and become less prominent. They are called stretch marks and tend to stay, getting fainter over the years.

At times you may be troubled with piles after childbirth. You might feel itchy around the anus. When piles are greatly aggravated they may even bleed. If you splash the anal area with cold water and then dab it dry, it will relieve the itching. Avoid spicy foods. A number of women have found the internal and external application of the ointment Procto Sedyl very comforting.

You must make sure you do pelvic floor exercises as described in the postnatal exercises, so that you regain the tone of those muscles and do not end up losing control of passing urine, or slackening of these muscles.

Although you will lose some weight at birth, it will take some time to regain your figure. Give yourself

8 months to a year. If you are considerably overweight you will have to work at it. At birth your weight loss will be equivalent to the weight of the placenta, the baby, the amniotic fluid. Over the weeks following the birth you will lose a lot of extra fluid content of your body.

**A sling for the baby**

REEF KNOT

Knot a dupatta of 2½ metres with a reef knot.

Sling the looped dupatta over your shoulder.

It will look like this from the back

Push the cloth inside out to create sling for the baby.

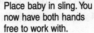

Place baby in sling. You now have both hands free to work with.

Older babies can be made to sit in the sling

# Exercises after a Normal Delivery

When you lie down to exercise, always do so without a pillow.

---

*Exercise 1*                                    *Days 1 & 2*

Lie on your back with knees bent, feet resting on the bed. Breathe in slowly and deeply, breathe out. Do this every day, between each exercise and at the end.

Do 5 times.

### Exercise 2

Lie with your legs straight and slightly apart. Bend and stretch your toes. Bend and stretch your ankles. Roll your feet round in circles in both directions. Do 5 times in each direction.

Repeat this 5 times.

### Exercise 3

Lie on your back with knees bent and feet resting on the bed. Tighten your buttock muscles and pull in your abdomen so that your back is pressed against the bed. Hold this position while you count 6, then relax.

Do 5 times.

Exhale and repeat, always exhaling before you start.

**Day 3**     Repeat the above exercises and add exercise 4, which will strengthen the muscles supporting the womb and help keep it in its right position.

### Exercise 4

This can be done sitting or lying down. Exhale, pull up the muscles through which your baby was born, thus tightening your vaginal muscles, i.e. you contract just as you would when you try to stop the flow of urine. Hold the contraction while you count 6; then relax. Exhale. Repeat.

Do 5 times, always exhaling before you start.

**Days 4 to 7**     Exercise 5

Lie with your right knee bent, and right foot on bed, left leg straight.

Slide your straight leg (left) down the bed, as far as possible, then slide the whole leg up the bed.

Only your waist muscles must work. Repeat with the other leg. Do 4 times with each leg.

*Exercise 6*
Lie with knees bent and feet on bed.

Draw in your abdominal muscles, reach across your body to place one hand on the opposite side of the bed, in level with your hips. Return to the starting position. Now do this with the other hand. Do a total of 8 times.

In the afternoon sleep on your stomach. Take a pillow under your head and one below your breasts to avoid discomfort.

## After a Caesarean Section

After the birth of your baby by abdominal surgery under general anesthesia you will be on the intravenous drip for some hours. The first thing to strike you after you come out of general anesthesia could be the discomfort of your abdominal scar. You would then be introduced to your baby. If you do some deep breathing, as much as you can comfortably manage, it will help to exhale the anesthesia out of your tissues and make you feel better.

It is common after a surgery to feel that you have a collection of mucus in your throat. Some women say

'I have just developed a bad throat.' The discomfort in the throat is caused as a result of a rubber tube inserted in your wind pipe during surgery, so that if you vomit while under anesthesia you do not inhale it into your lungs. It may cause a lot of dryness in the throat and make you want to cough. If you feel dryness in your throat, cover your mouth with a wet towel as you breathe, or/and put a couple of drops of water in your mouth to prevent dryness. When dryness does not bother you any longer, suck some cough drops or rock sugar *(mishri)* to soothe the throat.

The sooner you cough up the phlegm from your throat, the better you will feel. You have to learn to cough in your throat like singers before a vocal recital. Clear your throat and cough out. This will be more effective than taking cough syrup. The sooner the throat gets cleared, the better you will feel. While pregnant, practise coughing in your throat rather than from your abdomen.

The internal stitches on your abdomen will dissolve, but the external stitches may need to be removed a week to 10 days later. On the other hand, the external stitches may also be the dissolving kind. You will have to take it easy to allow the healing to take place.

On the 2nd day the nurse will come to change the sheets of your bed. It will be better if you get out of bed while she does so. Sit up in bed, by having your bed shifted to a sitting position. Place palms on either side of your body and lift your body up and gradually move yourself to the edge of the bed. Gently swing legs off the bed on the footstool or floor, hold a pillow in front of the abdomen for support, stand up and go to sit on a sofa/chair. Go gently back to bed when it is made. The whole exercise will make you feel much better by the end of it, since it will give an impetus to blood circulation.

If your first delivery is by a Caesarean section for a non–recurring factor like a failed induction or fetal distress, then the second delivery could be a normal delivery. If the first delivery is by Caesarean section from a recurring factor like a malformed pelvis, then the second delivery will also be by Caesarean section. Once you have had a Caesarean, all future labours should take place in a hospital. A uterus with a scar is watched carefully throughout pregnancy and labour. Rupture of the uterus is a serious but rare complication, occurring only in 0.5% of cases. Signs to be watched for are fresh, unusual vaginal bleeding, and pain over the scar.

*Exercises before stitches are removed*

The following are gentle exercises to be done after a Caesarean section.

*Exercise 1*

Lie on your back. Breathe in slowly and deeply, breathe out. Do 5 times, at least twice a day.

*Exercise 2*

Lie with your legs straight and slightly apart. Bend and stretch your ankles. Bend and stretch your toes. Roll your feet round in circles in both directions. *(see p.160)*

*Exercise 3*

Can be done sitting or lying down. Exhale, pull up the muscles of the pelvic floor, thus tightening your vaginal muscles, i.e. you contract just like you would when you try to stop the flow of urine. Hold the contraction till you count 6, then relax. Exhale. Repeat. Do 5 times, always exhaling before you start. *(see p.160)*

**Exercises after removal of stitches**

Exercises after the removal of the stitches on the7th and 8th day after a Caesarean section and for the same days after a normal delivery when you are up and about all day.

*Exercise 1*

Stand with legs crossed at ankles, press thighs, contract between the legs as you would when you tried to stop the flow of urine, pull in the abdomen and also tighten buttocks and anus. Hold it all tight for a count of 4, then relax. Repeat 6 times, always exhaling before you start.

*Exercise 2*

Stand with your back against the wall. Tighten buttock muscles and pull in the abdominal wall and try to get the lower part of your back and your entire backbone to touch the wall. (This exercise can also be done lying on the bed, same as Exercise 3, after a normal delivery.)

Repeat 6 times, always exhaling before you start.

*Exercise 3*

Standing, pull one leg up at the hip so that one leg is shorter than the other. Keep the knee straight as you do this, and lift foot off the ground. Repeat with the other leg. Do 4 times, and build up to 8 times. (Can be done lying down as in Exercise 5 after a normal delivery.)

*Exercise 4*

Stand with feet together, knees together, thighs pressed together. Move along the floor as if twisting for a short distance. Do once.

164

These simple exercises done for the first 40 days will do your figure miles and miles of good which even strenuous workouts later will not be able to achieve.

*Exercise 5*

After breastfeeding is completed, or when breast feeding is minimal towards the end, say 2 or 3 feeds a day, do bust exercise. (see p. 84)

## Bleeding / Sex

After the birth of the baby vaginally, or after a Caesarean section you will have a longish period lasting a week or several weeks (may be 4 to 6 weeks). Thereafter you may not have a period for several months, especially if you are breastfeeding.

The first period that occurs is usually longer and heavier than a normal period. It could last 7 days or more. Thereafter your regular cycle will set in. When the first period occurs is totally unpredictable. With breastfeeding it could come after 3 to 4 months, or after 6 to 9 months. In women who do not breastfeed, the period could start on the 28th day after the birth of the baby. The post–delivery discharge could be brownish/pinkish/occasionally red (when exertion is undertaken).

Not having a period need not mean that you are pregnant. Neither does it mean that since you are not getting a period you cannot become pregnant. You must use some contraceptive in consultation with your doctor. As soon as you feel you have healed vaginally, you can resume intercourse. This might take 10 days or so. Some women like to wait up to 40 days or 6 weeks. You can use some lubricant like petroleum jelly if required.

When you go to the doctor for a checkup you must inform him or her of any discomfort you might have with your bowel movement, passing of urine, sexual intercourse, or piles. Pelvic or pelvic floor discomfort would also need investigation.

You may walk up and down the stairs, but not more than is absolutely essential, that is, keep it to a minimum. Get as much rest as possible. Sleep for 2 hours in the afternoon. Go back to bed after the early morning feed at 5 to 6 a.m.

## Post-natal Depressions

It is common to have mood swings after the birth of the baby. Some women feel positive while others might feel negative.

When a woman is overly depressed, it is called post-partum psychosis. A woman suffering from post-partum depression will cry easily, sleep with difficulty, be tired and irritable, experience fear or a feeling of inferiority or inadequacy.

At times a woman feels resentful that from being a pampered pregnant woman she is now a responsible mother. Depression may also creep in when you feel depressed about the kind of birth experience you have had, or when you are overburdened with work and have no help to tide over this physically taxing phase in your life.

Occasionally the reality of babycare might be overwhelming. One mother helplessly exclaimed, 'But my baby smells shitty and vomity.' Your baby simply does not look and smell like the advertisements suggest. It will be better if you do not discuss your feelings with unsympathetic persons. But do discuss them with a trusted friend. It is healthy not to bottle up these negative emotions. Take things easy, do not worry too much about housework. There is no harm if things go unattended for a short while.

If depression persists consult a sympathetic doctor, whether your family physician or a homoeopathic doctor. Alternatively, you can consult a psychologist or psycho-therapist. Discussing your feelings with them will help tremendously in removing a psychological knot in your mind and unblock a lot of energy, so that you will feel and function better.

Depression can occur in a perfectly healthy woman. It might be caused by a sudden withdrawal of hormones from your body after the birth of the baby. The doctor might prescribe some artificial hormones for a while, the dosage of which he will gradually taper off. Alternatively, the doctor may prescribe anti-depressant drugs.

Most women have responded very well to homoeopathic medicines. In case postnatal depression does occur, women who take homoeopathic medicines tide over it quickly and effectively.

# 14. Contraception

In order to understand contraception it is important to understand how pregnancy takes place. For pregnancy to take place, an ovum or egg is released by one of the ovaries in the woman's body. When it is fertilised by a sperm, pregnancy begins. The release of the ovum in the woman's body is called ovulation.

Sperms are contained in the semi-gelatinous seminal fluid of the male ejaculation, which is slightly alkaline. Unless sperms gain access to the mouth of the womb or the cervix within 15 to 20 minutes following ejaculation, they are killed by the acid medium of the vagina. The cervix has an alkaline environment, so that sperms rapidly swim through it, up into the womb, and past the womb, along the fallopian tubes. In the fallopian tubes the ovum is fertilised. This journey takes 45 minutes. Sperms can survive and fertilise the ovum for approximately 2 days. Sometimes they can survive for 7 days. After being fertilised, the ovum takes 7 days to travel the length of the fallopian tube and reach the womb or uterus.

| | |
|---|---|
| *Abstinence* | The only sure way of not conceiving is to avoid intercourse altogether. However, this may be quite bad for your relationship with your husband. |
| *Coitus interruptus or the Withdrawal Method* | It is a method in which the penis is withdrawn before ejaculation. It requires a great amount of self-control by the man. Besides, sperms are present even in the leakage preceding ejaculation, and, from the region of the vulva where they may be deposited they can enter the vagina even when penetration does not take place. From the vagina they can enter the uterus and end up fertilising an ovum, leading to pregnancy. This is |

therefore a very unreliable method and should not be depended upon.

This is a natural method of birth control. For it to be successful it is important to pinpoint the time of ovulation, that is, the release of the ovum by the ovary, and its subsequent fertilisation. Ovulation generally occurs 14 days before the onset of the next period. If the ovum is not fertilised in approximately 18 hours it dies.

*Rhythm Method*

The first requirement of the use of this method is a regular cycle of periods occurring at regular and fixed intervals. The next step is to pinpoint the 14th day before the next cycle. If the periods occur at irregular intervals, it will be difficult to pinpoint this day. The exact timing of ovulation may vary slightly.

Sometimes shock, tension, or strain can further interfere with ovulation, causing it to occur anywhere from the 11th to the 17th day before the next cycle. Also, a perfectly predictable menstrual cycle may become irregular as a result of travel, strain, illness, in the age group of late 30s or early 40s, or after childbirth. During such times the method is unreliable.

In a regular 28 day cycle, it is not possible for conception to occur in the first 8 days of the menstrual cycle, beginning from the first day of the onset of the menstrual bleeding. So if there are 5 days of bleeding, 3 days after the bleeding are safe. Then the fertile period would be from the 9th to the 17th day, both days inclusive. From the 18th to the 28th day would again be a safe period.

In a woman with a 35 day cycle, the fertile period would be from the 15th to the 25th day, both days inclusive.

The rhythm method presupposes a perfectly regular cycle.

Another pitfall of the rhythm method is, that occasionally ovulation maybe provoked by sexual stimulation, regardless of the time of the fertile or non-fertile phase of the menstrual cycle.

Some lucky women find that this method works for them. They are very strict with their calculations and self-control. It may be a problem for women whose husbands tour a lot and happen to be home on the wrong days of the month. Besides it does not always work.

Added to the rhythm method, for greater accuracy one can follow the temperature method. Before ovulation a woman's body temperature dips slightly and when ovulation occurs, it rises slightly. A dip in the temperature signifies that the ovum is ready for release. A rise signifies the release of the ovum.

| | |
|---|---|
| *Temperature Method* | The temperature dips by just about 1 degree below the normal body temperature, and rises by just 1 degree above the normal body temperature on the Fahrenheit thermometer. It rises ½ a degree on the Centigrade thermometer scale. The temperature should therefore be taken by a very sensitive thermometer. After rising, the temperature remains high for 2 weeks, until the next period begins. A daily record has to be kept. It has to be tried for at least 6 months in order to be understood and followed accurately. If you are suffering from a fever or infection, the temperature reading will not be accurate. |

The temperature has to be taken at the same time every day. It has to be taken when you wake up in the morning, before getting out of bed and before taking food and drink. The thermometer must be left in place for at least 3 minutes.

The temperature reading could vary according to your menstrual cycle, the shortest cycle being 21 days and the longest 45 days. In a 28 day cycle the temperature would rise on approximately the 14th day after the first day of the menstrual period. In a 37 day cycle the temperature would rise on the 22nd day after the first day of the menstrual period.

If your temperature reading does not show the kind of reading mentioned here, continue to keep the record nevertheless. It would be of interest to your doctor as and when you go for consultations.

Vaginal secretions change during your cycle. A few days after your menstrual period you may notice a thick, cloudy and sticky mucus secretion. Around the time of ovulation it will change to clear, stretchy and abundant mucus. This attracts the sperm and allows easy penetration of it to fertilise the ovum. After the fertility period is over, the mucus again becomes thick, gelatinous and hostile to sperms.

*Checking the cervical mucus or the Billings Method*

To test vaginal secretions, you must first wash your hands with soap, then insert your finger in the vagina in order to get a sample of the secretions. Notice the nature of the secretions. It will take you a few months to accurately understand the secretions. Besides, sometimes semen may mask the true nature of your vaginal secretions. This method is also undesirable because it can cause vaginal infection and the mucus secretions cannot be accurately interpreted by the layman.

If your baby is 100% breastfed, it will change the levels of hormones in your body and prevent ovulation. That is, if you are demand-feeding your baby with no complementary bottles or other foods, a high level of prolactin hormone in your body will suppress ovulation. Breastfeeding also delays the onset of your next period. If you breastfeed on demand in the first few months, your period can take 6 to 8 months to return. If you add

*Breastfeeding*

171

complementary bottles and other foods to the baby's diet, your period could return in 2 to 4 months. On the other hand, when breastfeeding is continued unrestrictedly, your periods may take a year or more to return.

Even when you do not have a period, you could ovulate and become pregnant. On the other hand, some women may have a period or two that may be anovular, that is, not accompanied by ovulation, or a release of the egg. Hence breastfeeding and menstruation are unreliable indexes to whether you can conceive or not.

Along with breastfeeding if you take the progestogen–only pill or the mini–pill, it will help prevent conception, since it will be combined with reduced fertility produced by breastfeeding. You should not have the regular oestrogen–progestogen combined pill, since it will reduce milk production and have other undesirable side effects. When you go for a check up 6 weeks after delivery, tell the doctor you are breastfeeding and ask for advice. If you have intercourse before the 6-week period, you must use some other contraceptive, like the condom for instance.

The pill has one disadvantage. Its hormones are secreted in the milk and studies are continuing to find out if they have any ill effects on the baby. If you find that after taking the pill your baby has become irritable and not gaining weight as before, go off the pill and try some other contraceptive.

A breastfeeding woman should start the pill about 21 days before she plans to start weaning her baby on supplementary foods. If her period does not come after the first course of tablets, she should wait 7 days and start the next course of tablets. A period will come after weaning has been completed.

---

*Pills*    Pills are made of a combination of the 2 hormones, oestrogen and progestogen. The modern contraceptive pill has approximately 10% of the dose of hormone as compared to the pill in use 20 years ago. As a result the side effects are fewer and less severe. The hormones in the pill suppress the production of eggs by the ovaries by fooling them into believing that you are already pregnant. The pill is easily available in the market under brand names of Ovral-L, Triquilar, Mala D, Lyndiol, etc.

Since the hormonal dosage is greatly reduced, breakthrough bleeding sometimes occurs as a result of hormonal imbalance. In the first few days or the first few cycles of taking the pill, bleeding occurs. The blood loss usually occurs around the 17th day of the cycle and continues for a few days or until the next period. It appears in the form of spotting. The pills should be continued nevertheless. However, if it recurs, inform your doctor. It is possible that the doctor will change it to a pill with a higher hormone level to prevent further bleeding.

The pill should not be taken by young women whose bone growth is still not completed and who have not yet reached physical maturity. It should also be avoided by women above 35 years of age, women who smoke, those who have suffered from malignant disease, liver dysfunction, cardiac disease, kidney disease, diabetes, mental depression, epilepsy, or those having a previous history of thromboembolic manifestations or thrombophlebitis (problems with the clotting of the blood), bronchial asthma, or migraines.

When taken, it is important that it is taken at the same time every day. Its advantage is that it is the most efficient means of contraception. The failure rate is nil. It does not interfere with the spontaneity of sexual intercourse, and does not involve any mechanical device. It controls the menstrual cycle to 28 days, and reduces the amount of menstrual flow. It also eliminates or controls menstrual pain.

Just as some people are sensitive to certain drugs, e.g. some kinds of antibiotics, in the same way some women are sensitive to the pill. The possible side effects of the pill are nausea, fluid retention, weight gain, enlarged and painful breasts, change in sexual desire, and fungus infection of the vagina. Should any of these symptoms arise, you can discuss with your doctor whether you want to continue with the pill or switch to another contraceptive.

If on the pill, it is a good idea to take a break from it every 6 months. For 2 months use some other contraceptive and then get back to the pill. Allow 2 to 3 months to pass before becoming pregnant, so that you are sure that all the hormones have passed out of your system before you conceive. You will also be able to date your pregnancy more accurately.

The pill does not reduce fertility or your chances of conceiving, as is commonly believed. It is just that a woman who is already infertile may be taking it, and she becomes aware of her infertility only after she stops taking it.

The pill reduces the level of Vitamin $B_6$ folic acid, calcium, manganese, zinc and ascorbic acid in your body. It is therefore a good idea to take multi-vitamins along with it.

*The Intra Uterine Device (IUD)*

The intra-uterine device is a tiny device with a copper coil that can be inserted into the uterus during a vaginal examination, and left there. It can be inserted 6 weeks after the birth of the baby, after a normal delivery. The copper in this device makes the cervical mucus thick. Copper also makes the uterine lining hostile to the implantation of the fertilised ovum.

Although the success rate with the IUD is high, it is not

100 percent reliable, since it is only a mechanical hindrance to pregnancy. Should pregnancy occur and you decide to keep it, the IUD will be left inside. There is the possibility that the IUD may not be there at all. That is, you might have lost it, without realising it. If it is there, it can get embedded in the placenta, and be delivered with it after the birth of the baby or discharged with the period-like discharge after the birth of the baby. Should you decide to go for a medical termination of pregnancy, it should definitely be done within 12 weeks after the 1st day of the last menstrual period. During the abortion, the IUD will also be removed.

There are various brands of IUDs available such as Copper T, the Copper-7, and the Mutiload. If the insertion of the IUD does not suit a woman, that is, if it gives rise to profuse bleeding or pain, it can be removed and then re-inserted after 2 to 3 months. The first few periods after its insertion may be heavy. This may not matter in some cases. However, if a woman already has heavy periods or is anaemic, it may not be advisable.

Copper T

It is not advisable for a woman who has not had any children to use an IUD. IUDs have been known to cause perforation of the uterus, septic abortion, pelvic inflammation and ectopic pregnancy. Women with fibroids in the uterus or a prolapsed uterus should avoid the IUD.

In the case a normal delivery it can be inserted after 6 weeks, and 3 months after a Caesarean delivery. Otherwise it is preferable to insert it 2 to 3 days after the period is over. It could also be inserted during a period, or 6 weeks after a medically carried out or natural abortion.

After insertion it will give you a 2–to–3–year holiday from worries of contraception since that is how long it will remain effective. It is therefore a good device to be

Copper 7

used between pregnancies, to space children. If pregnancy is desired before that period, it can be removed as easily as it is inserted. It does not interfere with breastfeeding, nor does it introduce hormones into a woman's body. It can be removed as and when another pregnancy is desired.

A woman who has had an IUD inserted must make sure she has it removed after its effectiveness has dissipated.

## Condom

The condom is a rubber sheath that is placed over the erect penis before penetration. It works by preventing the sperm from entering the vagina. Various kinds are available in the market under brand names like *Nirodh*, *Masti*, *Kohinoor*, etc. If it is lubricated and freed of air before use, it is less likely to burst inside the vagina.

Sometimes it is not very effective because sperms may be deposited on the vulva before it is put on, through mild leaking from the penis that may take place earlier. Its efficacy depends on the care with which it is used. Used with a soluble spermicidal pessary in the vagina can greatly reduce its failure rate.

Condom

Some men do not like the condom as it takes away part of the sensation or because of the interference it brings into lovemaking, taking away spontaneity. However, used with care along with vaginal pessaries when other contraceptive methods are not available, it is very valuable. It also reduces the chances of catching sexually transmitted diseases, including the deadly disease AIDS.

## Diaphragm or the Cervical Cap

These are cones made of rubber with metal at the rim. They are fitted by the woman inside her body, in the vagina, over the cervix before intercourse and kept inside for 6 to 8 hours after intercourse. Along with them spermicidal creams have to be used. They have to be fitted by medical personnel for the correct size, and kept clean to avoid infection. Diaphragms, cervical caps, and spermicidal creams are not easily available in India.

Spermicidal pessaries are easily available in India under the brand name *Today*. It should be inserted into the vagina at least 4 to 5 minutes before intercourse and its contraceptive effect lasts for up to 1 hour. It can be used by itself, or together with the condom. It is more effective when used with the condom, since it must be at the cervix, not only somewhere in the vagina, when the sperm reaches the cervix or the mouth of the womb. The manufacturer's instructions should be followed carefully. Some women do not like the wetness of it.

*Spermicidal Pessaries*

This method should not be resorted to regularly. It is only to be used in emergencies. An IUD (intra-uterine device) fitted up to 7 days after sexual intercourse can prevent implantation of the fertilised egg in the womb. Although this will prevent a pregnancy, women often complain of a lot of pain and some bleeding.

*Morning after contraception*

Also, high dose morning-after pills can be had from a doctor or a family planning clinic. The pills are the ordinary combined oestrogen-progestogen contraceptive pills, not the mini-pill. A woman should take 2 of these pills as soon as possible and another 2½ hours later. These pills have to be taken within 72 hours or 3 days of the intercourse. There generally is nausea and vomiting after it. Some women might also experience headache, dizziness, and tender breasts.

Surgical sterilisation of the female is called tubal ligation or tubectomy. During the operation the fallopian tubes which carry the egg from the ovary to the womb are tied and cut, or alternately rings and clips are fixed on the fallopian tubes to block the passage of the egg from the ovary to the womb. It requires general anesthesia

*Surgical sterilization: female*

177

and a stay at the hospital for 2 to 3 days. If you have rings or clips on the fallopian tubes, the operation is more easily reversible. However, when getting it done, one should consider it as being irreversible. If during the operation the tubes get injured and bleed uncontrollably, they would be cut. When the tubes are cut or removed, reconstruction in order to make the surgery reversible will be impossible. Careful thought should be given to the idea before getting it done.

Apart from convalescence after the operation, it has no side effects. Periods, intercourse, menopause and sexual desire remain unchanged. In very rare cases women have been known to become pregnant after this surgery.

## Surgical sterilization: male

Surgical sterilisation of the male is called vasectomy. It is a simple operation. The tubes which carry the sperm from the testes to the penis are cut and tied. It is a minor surgery needing 15 to 30 minutes and can be carried out under a local anesthetic. If it is carried out under a general anesthetic the patient will need to stay in the hospital for a day.

It is a much simpler operation as compared with female sterilisation. It has the further advantage of being reversible in 70% of the cases. However, like female sterilisation, it should be regarded as irreversible.

After the operation there are no side effects, no change in sexual desire, strength or intercourse. If the man feels any change of sexual feelings, the problem is purely psychological. The man ejaculates as before, only the fluid will not contain any sperm. Following a vasectomy, sperms are still present in seminal fluid for some weeks. Contraception has to be used until the seminal fluid becomes spermfree. This would require a seminal analysis. When 2 consecutive analyses show an absence of sperms, only then can a man indulge in contraceptive-free intercourse.

Recently the government has approved of a medicine for abortion. It is not available over the counter at chemist shops. It is available with gynaecologists. It has to be taken within 49 days or 7 weeks of pregnancy, that is, about 19 to 20 days after a missed period. Before the medicine is given, the doctor will check and rule out an ectopic pregnancy. The medicine is made up of two drugs, one is an anti-pregnancy (anti-progesterone) drug and the other is an expulsive drug (prostoglandin). After it is given, bleeding starts and can continue for 7 to 10 days. After the bleeding stops, an ultrasound is done to make sure abortion is complete. In case of an incomplete abortion, a minor operation (D&C) will be performed. This medicine therefore can be had only where medical support and back-up are available. It has a 95% success rate. In 5% of cases when it fails, it has to be backed up by a D&C.

*Medicine For Abortion*

Various methods of contraception are currently being researched. However no ideal solution has yet been found.

*Contraception in the future*

Presently, research is taking place on vaccines or injections to prevent pregnancies; also on hormone implants under the skin in women, for contraceptive purposes; on hormone preparations that can be taken like snuff; on better quality condoms; on effective methods of pinpointing ovulation precisely, to help those who would like to use the rhythm method. The male pill has been tried and found to have too many negative side effects. There is also research on surgical insertion of a valve in the tubes of man and woman, to be removed as required at a later date. Who knows what course future contraception will take?

# 15. Breastfeeding

## Why should I breastfeed?

That is all you need! Breast milk is nutritionally balanced and easily available. It prevents disease in the baby. Best of all, it costs nothing, and is delivered according to consumer demand! It comes sterilised, and at the right temperature.

Breastfeeding helps the mother lose weight, and encourages her uterus to contract to its normal size and position. Incidence of breast and ovarian cancer, anaemia and osteoporosis tends to be lower in women who have breastfed.

Breastfeeding helps babies feel loved and secure. It encourages bonding.

The mother and the whole family can get better nutrition, whereas enormous amounts of money and energy are spent on bottle feeding.

Breastfed babies are more active.

Breast milk is best for the proper growth of the baby. It also helps the baby's brain development. In pregnancy, fat is deposited in the Mother's body to be used during feeding. Mother's milk has fat and lactose (carbohydrate) in it; so you lose weight faster than a woman who is bottle-feeding.

Breast milk also protects the baby from allergies, and from disease. Since breast milk is always pure, breastfed babies have fewer bowel upsets.

If you wear a good supportive bra while feeding, breastfeeding need not cause the breasts to sag. Breasts can also sag with age or obesity, without ever nursing a child.

181

## How does the Baby Feed ?

Wrong

The baby's gums press on the areola, that is, the dark area behind the nipple. The nipple gets extended back towards the baby's gullet, and the baby's tongue milks it, by pressing it against the roof of the baby's mouth or palate.

Right

If the baby munches on the nipple instead of the areola, it will hurt the mother. A major part of the areola will continue to be visible, and the baby will be dissatisfied because not much milk will come.

Since the baby has to munch for each sip of milk, its jaw development improves. Also, it makes it possible for the baby to pause in between, just to breathe or look around.

As opposed to this, a bottle-fed baby gets a continuous flow of milk through the bottle's nipple and tends to overeat. So the seeds of becoming overweight are sown right at the start.

## How to Feed

When the baby latches on to the breast to feed, and it hurts, it is possible the baby has not latched on properly. If the baby's gums press on the nipple it will hurt. If the baby's gums correctly press on the dark area behind the nipple, the baby's sucking will not cause any discomfort. Correct sucking releases the flow of milk, and causes relief to the mother, especially if the breasts are hard

*Signs of the Baby Being Latched On*

1. The muscle below the baby's ears moves as the baby sucks and swallows

2. The baby's chin touches the mother's breast

3. The lower lip curls outwards

4. More of the areola shows above the baby's upper lip and less under its lower lip.

and sensitive from being overfull. The release of
milk is accompanied by a tingling sensation of
the breasts.

If the baby's sucking hurts, insert a finger in
the baby's mouth, between the gums, to break
the suck. Then, in order to avoid the baby's
gums pressing on the nipple, put in more of the
breast, so that correct latching on takes place,
and the baby's gums press on the areola, the
dark area behind the nipple, instead.

To do so, stroke the baby's cheek towards the
side you want to feed from. The baby will turn
with the mouth open to that side. Quickly pull
the baby very close to you, so that the baby can
latch on correctly.

Feeding the colostrum and foremilk helps to
teach the baby how to suck, so that when the
milk comes in, sucking brings relief to the
mother.

If the colostrum is not given to the baby, and
instead sugared water or bottle milk is repeatedly fed,
the baby will get used to getting a constant flow from
the bottle's nipple without having to suck very
much.

After a few days, when milk comes in, the breasts
are painful and sensitive. A baby who has had the
colostrum will relieve this discomfort by sucking at the
breast and emptying it. But a baby who has not sucked
at the breast before will take time to learn; and during
this learning process, cause considerable discomfort to
the mother.

If the baby feeds entirely on one breast at one feed and
on the next breast at the other feed, it gets the fat rich

hindmilk which makes the mother lose weight and the baby put on weight. It also thoroughly empties both breasts. The baby takes 20 to 30 minutes of suckling to empty one breast. If the baby is still hungry, you could feed it from the other side briefly. Start the next feed from the side you fed briefly from.

## Breast Size

The size of breasts in no way determines success or failure when feeding. Women with fairly small breasts can feed as efficiently as women with large breasts.

During pregnancy you will put on a 1–1½ kg weight on the breasts, and as pregnancy advances you will need a larger sized bra. The size could increase by two sizes, that is, a woman normally wearing size 34 could need size 38 as she goes past her 6th month.

After the baby is born, when the milk comes into the breast after a few days, the breasts become big, heavy and uncomfortable. In the first 2 to 3 months, the breasts will remain fairly large. At times hardness and fullness may also be experienced when the baby skips a feed.

After 8 to 12 weeks the breasts will go back to their normal size and feel soft, just as they were before pregnancy. This does not mean that you are no longer producing milk. You might still be feeding the baby, but this time the supply and demand balance is just right, and no overproduction of milk, or overfilling of breasts takes place.

When feeding goes on for many months, some women might find their breasts going smaller than before they became pregnant. It will take them time

*Types of Nipples*

to put on the fat again and to
regain their original size.

## Flat Nipples

If your nipples do not project
as nipples normally do, and
appear flat or dimpled, they
are called flat or inverted

Inverted    Flat    Normal    Long

nipples. Being flat, your nipples may project when you
are cold, sexually aroused or when feeding the baby.

Flat nipples are no longer considered
to be a problem. As the baby suckles,
a nipple-like shape gets formed with
the area of the nipple and part of the
areola. Lack of projection of the nipple
when the baby sucks could make the
baby unable to grasp it in its mouth.

**The Syringe Method**
(Nirmala Kesaree Method)
You need:
A 10ml syringe and a blade

Remove plunger and cut the end on which the
needle is inserted with the blade.

Replace the plunger through the cut side.

Place the uncut side of the syringe on the
breast and gently pull the plunger to help the
nipple project.

If that is the case, the syringe
method can be used to encourage
the nipple to project.

Once projectivity is achieved, the
syringe is removed and the baby
quickly put to the breast. Also
expressing milk will make it easier
for the baby to grasp the areola.

In case the baby has a problem
grasping the nipple during a feed,
express some milk from the breast
first, so that it becomes softer and
easier for the baby to grasp.
Expression can be done by hand or
by a breast pump. When offering
the breast, both the nipple and areola

must be put well into the baby's mouth. Once the baby has latched on, the nipple will remain projected for the rest of the feed. Also, after manual expression of milk, if one drop of milk is left on the tip of the nipple, it will act as an appetizer for the baby.

## Breastfeeding at Birth

If the baby is simply held in a relaxed manner, close to the mother's breast within 30 minutes after birth, it will latch on to the mother's breast and start suckling. This is because babies are born with 3 reflexes:

- **Homing in reflex:** the baby moves towards the areola,

- **Rooting reflex:** the baby attaches itself to the mother's breast for feeding.

- **Sucking reflex:** the baby sucks at the breast.

If and when the baby is breastfed at birth, it immediately learns how to attach itself to the breast and does not struggle to do so after the breast gets filled with milk. Besides it gets some colostrum, which however little, will protect it from infections.

Breastfeeding at birth also promotes bonding. According to J.C. Pearce in his book *Magical Child* (1980), 'Bonding is stage specific. Nature has designed the bonds to be established in the hours immediately following birth... as is the

### Baby-friendly Hospitals

Some hospitals are labelled baby–friendly hospitals if their policies encourage breastfeeding. In such hospitals, the resident doctors, consultant and labour room staff encourage breastfeeding of new born, within half an hour in a normal delivery, and within 4 to 6 hours after a Caesarean delivery. Such hospitals also avoid the routine use of sedatives or analgesics which could lead to a depression in the infant and interfere with the normal sucking reflex of the baby at birth.

The health care staff in these hospitals should inform the mother of the advantages of exclusive breastfeeding and the disadvantages of artificial feeding. All newborns in such hospitals are routinely kept with the mother 24 hours a day. The baby's cot would therefore be in the mother's room, next to her bed.

It is essential for baby–friendly hospitals to display their breast-feeding policy document in the antenatal clinic, maternity ward, special care nursery, etc.

case of learning to breathe, this is a critical period for bonding.'

J.C. Pearce further explains that when the mother breastfeeds her baby at birth she stimulates all the 5 senses of the baby, that is, touch, smell, sight (the baby can concentrate on a face 6 to 12 inches away from its own in the hour following birth), taste and hearing (since most mothers will 'talk' to the baby while feeding). This in turn stimulates the reticular formation of the brain, (an area of the brain that receives messages from the 5 senses). It gives the baby better coordination between the brain and the 5 senses for the rest of its life.

When this happens, 'All adrenal steroid production has completely disappeared in a short time because the infant, in being returned to, and recognising the known, relaxes. He then remains in an alert and yet calm state of learning.'

## Rooming In

It is best for the mother to have her baby with her in her room and feed it on demand. Initially, before breast milk comes in, the colostrum being heavy will make the baby sleep long hours without demanding a feed. This gives the mother the rest she needs. Further, colostrum and breast milk give the baby immunity or protection from infections in the hospital and from visitors.

Each one of us has some bacteria or germs on our body. When the baby is next to the mother, it develops a bacterial flora that is similar to that of the mother. When the child is in the nursery, it can catch the bacterial flora of the nurse, who may be carrying some infection, or may not wash her hands before touching

> ## Stools of Breastfed Babies
>
> Breastfed babies normally pass very frequent stools, that are not wholly formed. Sometimes with wind, a bit of stool may be passed. Bottlefed babies pass harder stools which may give rise to constipation.

the baby. Plus, instead of getting the mother's immunity rich, infection fighting colostrum, the baby may receive a bottle of milk, which will make it further susceptible to infections. It is therefore better for the baby to be with the mother.

Glucose water or bottle milk may sometimes be given as a 'test feed'. Interestingly, if this test feed is aspirated into the baby's lungs it can irritate the baby's lungs. Colostrum on the other hand if aspirated into the lungs will not irritate, but simply get absorbed.

If you are expecting lots of guests, you can put a notice on the baby's crib saying 'Please do not touch me.' Or else you could have the baby lie next to the mother on the bed and say the doctor has asked to keep the baby next to the mother. This is in fact an excellent thing to do with small babies, because they get the body heat of the mother, and the baby's own temperature control mechanism is not strained. Further you could put a notice, 'Please wash your hands before you hold me' or 'Please do not hold me if you are unwell.'

## Exclusive Breastfeeding

Feeding only breast milk is recommended for 6 months. That is, no other milk, water or mashed foods need to be given. There is enough water in the breast milk for the baby. The mother will need to drink lots of water and eat nutritious food when she is feeding.

## Constant Feeding Demand

Some babies want to be constantly fed. According to one mother, within 10 to 15 minutes her baby would want to be fed again. When put to the breast again, however, it did not suck properly, so she gave him the bottle. On enquiry it was revealed that breastfeeding was the only time she held her baby. So what the baby was demanding was not a feed, but comfort sucking. If a baby seems to be wanting constant feeding, it may not be asking for a nutritious feed, but comfort sucking. Abundant cuddling of the baby or strapping the baby on to the mother will reduce the baby's need to fake hunger, when, what it actually wants is simply to be held close and feel secure.

Another time a baby may want constant suckling is when it experiences a growth spurt. When the baby grows, it needs more milk. Feeding more often increases milk supply. So, if suddenly the baby seems to want more feeding, just take a couple of days off. Stay in bed, eat well, and feed on demand. Once the supply is stepped up, the baby will stop demanding constant feeding.

## Leaking Breasts

As breastfeeding gets established, the breast may start leaking milk after a bath. Or when the mother feeds from one side, the other side may leak. Sometimes when it is time for the baby's feed, or when the mother lovingly thinks of the baby, the milk starts leaking. It is better not to wear water proofed backed bra pads, since they cause the nipples to remain soggy and become sore. As the demand and supply settles down, leaking of breasts may reduce. You could fold some cotton in an absorbent men's hanky and place inside the bra to avoid your clothes getting wet from leakage when you have company. You could place an ever–dri baby nappy or a piece of blotting paper between the breast and the hanky to keep nipples from becoming soggy.

## Let Down Reflex

This is a reflex that causes milk to be 'let down' and flow when the baby is feeding. If the mother is worried, stressed, extremely self–conscious, etc., it can interfere with the release of milk. It is therefore important that a breastfeeding mother is relaxed, so that her milk can flow freely. If tension prevents the let down reflex or interferes with it, a mother can have a glass of wine or beer to relax herself. Wine and beer both have a low alcohol content, just enough to relax the mother. Moreover beer is known to aid lactation.

## Feeding When Ill

Cold, flu, fevers should not require you to stop feeding. However, do let the doctor know that you are nursing the baby, when he prescribes you medicines. Feeding should continue as long as possible, so that the baby can get the maximum advantage of the immunities present in the mother's milk. An infected mother produces within her body antibodies to fight the infection she has. These are secreted in breast milk. They become available to the baby and protect it against infection.

When feeding, antibiotics such as tetracycline and streptomycin, steroids and sulpha-containing drugs should be avoided.

Some laxatives may cause colic and diarrhoea in the baby. Anti thyroid drugs may cause goitre. Anti-coagulants and large doses of aspirin can cause bleeding problems in the baby.

Sedatives or tranquillisers such as valium can cause drowsiness and feeding problems.

190

# To Stop Feeding Suddenly

If, for some reason, you have to stop feeding abruptly, do it under your doctor's supervision. The doctor will give you a safe drug called bromocriptine that will dry up the milk. If you simply stop feeding abruptly, you may subject yourself to extreme discomfort. It is best to taper off feeding gradually.

*Every day, after the sixth month*

# Breast Preparation for Feeding

From the 6th month of pregnancy onwards, certain breast preparation techniques have to be started, to ready the breasts and nipples for feeding.

Because of the manner in which the baby sucks, it is important to toughen the mother's nipples so that they can avoid sore or cracked nipples.

With a dry towel, clean the tip of the nipples. You may find dry scabs falling off. Don't worry about it. At times drops of colostrum get secreted unnoticed and dry at the tip of the nipple, forming scabs or flakes.

Hold both nipples as you hold a cigarette, that is , between your forefinger and middle finger. Now draw it in and out or forward and backward 50 times. Hold nipple lightly. If you press with your fingers it can hurt.

Each time the baby sucks, its gums press on the dark area behind the nipple, and the nipple gets extended way back towards the baby's throat, from where milk goes straight down the baby's gullet. So, you are acquainting the

> **Precaution**
>
> If you have premature contractions or bleeding or have been prone to either and are on medication to prevent them, do not breast prepare after the sixth month of pregnancy. Instead, do it 15 days before the estimated date of delivery.

nipple with the action of feeding when doing this preparation.

If you like, this can be incorporated in your love life. That is, while making love your husband can suck at the breast.

Hold the areola, the dark area behind the nipple, between the forefinger and thumb, and press. Do it twice. You might notice a few drops of fluid appearing at the tip of the nipple. Don't worry if you do not notice any. It will appear gradually over the weeks.

Wipe off the drops of fluid and lightly apply any natural oil on the nipple and areola. You can use coconut oil, ghee or groundnut oil. Synthetic based oils, that is, petroleum based oils, are best avoided. Also, scented oils or vitamin enriched oils are to be avoided.

## When Feeding

The body has its own system of secreting lubrication from the Montgomery's tubercles (little prominences around the areola), to keep the nipple supple and oiled. However, during a bath when soap is used, it gets washed away, so women find rubbing oil useful. Continue to use coconut oil when feeding. That is, after a feed, apply a little oil on the nipple and areola, in a thin film. Before the next feed, clean the nipple and areola with a small piece of cotton soaked in water that has been boiled. So, keep bits of cotton soaked in a covered bowl of boiled water. Use a fresh piece of cotton for each breast. You are not only wiping out the oil, but also stale breast milk, perspiration, and threads from garments.

If you experience mild contractions when feeding, use your breathing for labour to deal with it. These are caused because feeding releases oxytocin hormone which contracts the uterus and helps it to involute to its normal size. Therefore involution of the uterus is more efficient when you breastfeed.

## Forerunner to milk

Towards the end of pregnancy, say in the last 3 months, women often notice a yellowish fluid escape from the breast. Even if they do not notice it, a few drops may appear and dry at the tip of the nipple, forming a crust or scab.

This is called colostrum, or foremilk. It is fed to the baby before the milk comes in. Milk might take 2 or 4 days to come in. For about 10 days it is still mixed with colostrum and looks rich and creamy. Earlier, colostrum was regarded as unclean milk, and mothers were forbidden from feeding it to the baby. This is yet another one of the old wives' tales which should be ignored. Feeding colostrum to the baby is full of advantages. It definitely must be fed to the baby.

## Colostrum

It has more proteins than mature milk but has less carbohydrates and fat. The protein gives the baby a full feeling, so that it remains satisfied longer after a feed, enabling it to sleep and rest for long periods in the first days of life. At the same time, it also gives the mother time to rest.

Antibodies are present in mother's mature milk; only there are many more in colostrum. Later the baby will produce its own antibodies, but in the first few months, it can't, and depends on its mother for them.

193

These antibodies protect the baby from a number of bacterial and viral infections that the mother may have suffered from or has been immunised against, among these being pneumonia, whooping cough, E-coli gastroenteritis, typhoid, flu, dysentery, tetanus etc. Although the extent of protection received by the baby may at times be complete and at other times only partial, it is very important for the baby to get these antibodies from colostrum and mother's milk, until its body can manufacture its own antibodies, or during what is called the immunity gap.

Colostrum contains minerals like zinc and calcium and Vitamins A, $B_6$, $B_{12}$ and E. It also has a laxative effect and helps the baby pass its first stool, which is black and sticky. It has a higher cholesterol content than milk, which may be important at this stage for promoting the growth of the nervous system, and possibly later in life for helping the body to cope with cholesterol.

## Mature Milk

The colostrum gradually changes into mature milk during the first few days. There is no sudden change. The more a baby feeds, the sooner milk will be produced in large amounts. If a mother is feeding her baby infrequently, it may not come until the 4th or 5th day.

In the meantime you have transitional milk, that is milky looking colostrum. Transitional milk changes into mature milk.

Mature milk is thinner looking, whiter or bluish white. In the first year of breastfeeding, the protein present in the milk gradually falls, regardless of the mother's diet. This is because the baby grows fastest in

194

the first 6 months when the protein content in breast milk
is the highest.

## Engorgement

A dramatic change occurs in the breasts when milk
comes in, a few days after delivery. The breasts become
larger than ever, hard, sensitive, full, and uncomfortable.
The change is due to the increased blood supply in the
breasts and the start of full milk production. This heavy
uncomfortable stage is known as engorgement and lasts
for 24 to 48 hours.

## How to Deal with Engorgement

If engorgement occurs, emptying the breast will
help to relieve the discomfort. In order to do
so, one must slightly oil the breast. Then, place
both hands against the chest and around the
breast and slowly slide hands down towards
the nipple. When the fingers reach the areola,
the dark area behind the nipple, press it with
the fingers in order to release some milk. After
pressing the areola from above and below,
continue to press from opposite directions and
go around the areola. Repeat several times on one
breast. Then follow the same procedure on the
other breast. You can keep a towel to collect the
drips.

Sometimes during engorgement the
baby might find it difficult to grasp the
nipple and areola. In that case the mother
can express some milk by pressing on the areola.
This will empty the breast slightly and make it easier for
the baby to grasp.

Cold compress used immediately after a feed will

195

prevent engorgement by causing the blood-vessels to contract. Alternatively a warm bath before a feed will soften the breast and help the nipple to stand out for feeding.

## To Express Breast Milk

To express milk, place the thumb and fingers as flat as possible on the spot where areola and breast meet, and press. After having pressed a few times, very gently move your finger and thumb together backwards towards the chest, so that you press on the wider milk ducts behind the areola also. Pressing in this way move your thumb and finger in a circle around the areola.

To manually express milk for collection, in order to be fed later to the baby, choose a time when you are not in a hurry. Wash your hands with soap and water and dry them on a towel kept aside for this purpose. Once the flow has begun, press on either side of the areola as illustrated. Soon after feeding the baby from one breast, you can express from the second breast. Or you could apply warmth to your breast by applying a warm towel before you begin to express. During expression milk comes out slowly. The flow is greater when the baby suckles.

Before feeding, expressed breast milk it should not be boiled. Just stand the bottle in hot water to warm the milk slightly and feed. While standing in the refrigerator, the milk may separate into fat and water layers; that does not mean it has gone bad. If the milk is not really chilled, there is no harm in feeding cold milk to the baby. If expressed milk is to be fed at night, express during the morning, when milk production is greater, after you have been nicely rested. Or express at night so that it

*Expressed Milk*

Expressed milk will stay unspoilt at room temperature for 6–8 hours even in the summer. It will stay in the refrigerator for 24 hours, and in the freezer for 1 to 3 months.

can be fed at noon, the next day. Alternatively keep collecting expressed milk by your bedside. It can be fed to the baby when required, for instance, if you sleep through a feed or are bathing when the baby wakes for a feed, or if you need to go out for a few hours. Every 8 hours discard the remaining milk and collect in a fresh sterilized glass.

Breast milk can also be expressed with a breast pump.

### *Expression through Breast Pumps*

#### *The bulb type*
This has a bulb of rubber and the rest is made of a glass funnel. First the rubber bulb is pressed and the glass funnel is placed over the nipple and areola. Then the rubber bulb is released. This creates a suction and consequent release of milk. The disadvantage of this pump is that the rubber bulb cannot be boiled for sterilisation. It should only be used to remove and discard milk.

---

#### *Precaution*
All equipment used for expression must be sterilised by boiling. If they are sterilised by soaking in a sterilising solution, they should be rinsed off with boiled water before use. Metal should not be put in a sterilising solution.

#### *The syringe type*
An imported breast pump kit that works on the same principle as a syringe. It is available at some major chemist shops in big cities.

#### The Battery operated type
This version is available for home use.
They work well when the breast is very full. They are the opposite of the manually operated ones.

#### The electric type
This is generally used in hospitals.

## How to Feed Expressed Breast Milk

Expressed breast milk could be fed either from a glass or with a cup and spoon to the baby.

> ### Hiccups
>
> Sometimes babies start hiccups after a feed. It is nothing to worry about, although some parents get anxious when they hear the baby's rather loud hiccups. It is normal and will pass.

When using a glass, a small glass with a round, smooth edge is good. It should not have a sharp edge.

A small *katori* (bowl) with a smooth edge can also be used. Put some expressed milk in the glass, cup or bowl. Place the baby with the head slightly raised on your lap. Place the edge of the bowl at the baby's lower lip and tilt till the level of milk reaches the lips of the baby. The baby will sense its presence and lap it up with the tongue like a puppy! When the level of the milk goes down, tilt some more. Initially, if given to a baby who has already had a bottle, the baby is likely to protest by flaying its arms. This might drop some milk, so make the baby wear a bib before trying it for the first time or ask someone to hold the baby's arms. The alternative would be to swaddle the baby or wrap it in a sheet so that its arms do not flay. Gradually the baby will become adept at it.

A traditional feeding cup or *paladi*

You could also feed the baby with a small spoon after positioning it on your lap as described above.

A *paladi* or traditional feeding cup can also be used.

As the baby grows, apart from expressed breast milk, soups, juices, water, milk or any other liquid can be fed in a similar way.

## If the Baby's Nose Gets Blocked

If engorgement causes the breasts to become very full and the soft breast tissue presses against the baby's nose, causing it to leave the breast in panic, do not press the breast down with a finger to free the baby's nose.

It will cause the nipple to project upwards, which in turn will lead to the nipple hitting against the roof of the baby's mouth and block the ducts on the tip of the nipple, or cause the nipple to get sore or cracked.

Instead of pressing the breast down, place all your fingers below the breast and lift the breast. Let the thumb be relaxed. This will cause a considerable part of the bulge to tilt towards the chest and meet the chest. It will also present the nipple at the right angle to the baby for feeding.

If the baby's nose is blocked because of a cold you could feed the baby expressed milk with a spoon or cup. Alternatively you can put a few drops of saline solution in the baby's nostrils to clear the block.

## Feeding Time

The baby should be fed as and when it demands a feed. Hospital routine may encourage breastfeeds by the clock. This regulated system is based on bottle feeding, and has no bearing on breastfeeding.

The letdown reflex or release of the flow of milk may take a few minutes to be established. It can be affected by embarrassment at nursing, fear of discomfort, contractions during feeding, etc. Hence, if the baby is removed too soon from the breast, the flow will be that much weaker.

In the first few days, the baby should be put to the breast as long as it likes, which could be 20 to 30 minutes at a time. The more complete the emptying of the breast, the more successful the establishment of lactation will be.

## Relax When You Feed

It is important to relax when you feed. If you do not relax, it will interfere with the letting down of milk, that is, the release of milk does not take place when you are tense.

It is therefore a good idea to retire to a quiet, undisturbed corner with your baby at feeding time. You can carry with you a tall drink to savour when feeding.

If you are tense when feeding, the baby will sense it immediately, and may not want to leave the breast as a result. It does not mean that it is hungry; what it is doing is sucking for comfort and security. So, it is important to relax.

If you have a problem with space, you can fix a curtain in front of your bed for privacy. Or, you can use a light scarf of net or georgette to cover yourself and your baby.

If you cannot help being tense, express your milk and feed it to the baby from a sterilised cup and spoon.

## Night-feeds

Newborn babies need to be fed frequently, because of their body weight and their fast rate of growth. Until the baby weighs around 10 pounds it will need to get up at night for a feed. Once the baby weighs 10 pounds it can sleep for about 5 hours without waking up with hunger.

Try and give the baby the last feed when you yourself go to bed at night. When the baby wakes up at night, you can feed the baby in bed, and let it drop off to sleep with you. Keep a nappy change, and a torch close at hand. Instead of a torch, you can keep a zero watt bulb switched on all night.

Do not delay the feed until the baby has cried itself hoarse. If the baby is allowed to cry when it is hungry, it will fray your nerves; besides, when put to the breast, the baby will feed only for a short while and fall off to sleep from exhaustion; only to wake up with hunger, after an hour or so.

So, when your baby wakes up for a feed at night, pick him/her up, or have your husband pass him/her to you. Your husband can help in this way, at least 3 times a week. Keep the room darkened. Do not play or otherwise distract the baby. Sing a lullaby, which should be sung only at bedtime. Let the baby learn to associate minimum activity with night time.

At least 3 times a week go to bed early if your baby regularly wakes up at night. Keep water by your bedside in case you get thirsty. If you find it difficult to go back to sleep, try to relax by totally letting go your body. Make sure you are comfortable. Being angry will not help. If you are very tired, you can express breast milk which can be fed to the baby by your husband through a cup or a cup and spoon. This will enable you to sleep through one feed and get 4 to 5 hours of undisturbed sleep. It is recommended that this is made routine since a mother who is well rested can cope better with the demands of motherhood. The baby will also relax if it senses the mother's relaxed mood.

# Foremilk and Hindmilk

The early part of a feed is made up of foremilk which is low in fat, while the latter part is the hindmilk, and has 4 to 5 times the amount of fat and 1½ times as much protein. Hence the foremilk is thin, whereas hindmilk is thicker.

Many hungry babies whose mothers think they are not producing enough milk, get only the thin, low calorie foremilk, and the mother stops feeding before the high fat hindmilk is consumed by the baby. As a result, the baby actually loses weight or fails to gain weight and is therefore started on cow's milk or powdered milk.

## Will My Milk Be Enough?

Since we cannot measure the number of ounces of milk a breastfed baby gets, many mothers wonder whether it is enough. Remember, it is Nature's food for the baby, the same Nature that nourished the baby inside the womb and made it form into a little human being. Your milk is the best suited to your baby's needs, much as cow's milk is best suited to a calf's needs.

To check if the baby is getting adequate nourishment, the doctor will weigh the baby when you go for a checkup. If your doctor says the baby is putting on weight normally, it is obvious that your milk is sufficient.

*How to Tell If Baby is Getting Enough Milk*

If a baby has 6 wet diapers in 24 hours, it is getting enough input, or milk. Besides, less volume of breast milk is needed as compared to other milk given in a bottle, because all of breast milk gets absorbed.

## Less Milk

If you feel you are producing less milk, all you have to do is feed more often. Each time you feed, the body releases prolactin hormones, which further stimulate the formation of milk.

If you skip a feed in the hope of storing more milk for the next feed, it will not work, for the less you feed, the more your milk supply will dwindle. The amount consumed at a feed can be determined by weighing the baby before and after a feed without a change of clothes. It you feel the milk is not enough, feed more often and persist. If you get panicky and mix breast with bottle, the battle is lost. It is also said that eating *jeera* or cumin seeds, *methi* or fenugreek seeds increases the production of milk. So does a glass of beer/wine a day.

You should check with your doctor about any medicine you take, even if it is an aspirin, just to make sure it will not affect the milk supply.

## Burping the Baby

Babies should be made to burp once or twice during a feed. The baby can burp once while being fed and at later the end of a feed. With the burp the baby could bring up some milk or curd.

Burping brings up any wind that has been swallowed during feeding or crying prior to feeding, so that it does not cause any discomfort to the baby. Babies vary a great deal in the amount of air they swallow, so some may burp immediately, while others take longer to burp. Bottle-fed babies swallow more air than breastfed babies. So do breastfed babies who gulp milk fast or cry while feeding. If not burped, the baby can become uncomfortable and restless. However, if the baby does not burp when held upright in order to be made to burp, and seems otherwise happy and satisfied, do not become particular about burping. Let it pass. Probably she/ he does not need burping since she/he has not swallowed much air.

If the baby falls asleep while having a feed, do not wake it for burping. Put it on its side. This position will cause the air to come up automatically. The milk it brings up with a burp will run out of its mouth and not bother it.

## How to Position the Baby

The most common position of a mother feeding a baby is sitting, with the baby supported by her arm, bent at her elbow. A pillow on the lap will provide support to the arm supporting the baby. The baby should be turned towards the mother's body. That is, the baby should be held tummy to tummy with the mother. The mother should take a back rest and sit with her back straight. It may not be possible for her to sit straight after the birth of the baby because her pelvic floor may still be uncomfortable because of the stitches. In that case she can use an inflated rubber ring (available at chemist shops for piles patients) to sit upon.

Alternatively, when the mother is tired at night, she can lie down on her side and feed the baby. It is important for the mother to be relaxed in whichever position she adopts. Secondly, the breast should fall towards the baby. If the breast is falling away from the baby, it will require the baby to tug at the nipple and may cause soreness or cracks in the nipples.

## Position After Caesarean Birth

If the baby has been delivered under general anesthesia, the mother is likely to be unconscious initially. As soon as the mother responds to commands, that is, if she is told to move to her right or left, she responds, she can commence feeding.

Within 24 hours or the 1st day of the birth of the baby, the baby can be placed on to the top of the mother for feeding.

204

In the next 24 hours or 2nd day after the birth, the mother can roll to her side and feed lying on her side.

Subsequently, on the 3rd day after birth the mother can be propped up to sit. A pillow can be placed on one side. The baby's body should turn towards the mother's body and taper off towards the side of the mother, below her arm.

## Twins

Twins can be fed one at a time, or together. When two babies suck at the breasts, the breasts produce enough milk to feed both.

You can feed twins 3 hourly rather than feeding them on demand. In the beginning, you can feed each baby separately, so that you can get to know them individually. You can feed them one after the other. Start with whoever wakes up first and then wake the other baby. Many twin babies develop a preference for their own breast. One baby might be an eager sucker while the other may be lazy.

## How to Position Twins

Place a pillow on your lap below the breast. Place the baby's head at the breast, and let the baby's body taper to the side of your body, the feet falling to the side of your waist, below your arm. Place the other baby on the other breast in a similar fashion.

Or else, you can place a baby in the usual way, that is, head at one breast, and the body tapering towards the other breast, and the second baby, with the body tapering towards the side of your body.

## Bonding

The more skin–to–skin contact your baby enjoys with your body when feeding the more strong a bond will develop between you and the baby. You should hold the baby against your bare skin when feeding.

If you haven't felt very motherly at birth, you are going to feel a gush of maternal affection as your baby gazes intently straight into your eyes when feeding. This is specially important if you have had a Caesarean birth.

Babies also tend to grasp your finger, or, when older, scratch your breast when feeding. As they feel relaxed and satisfied at the breast, they begin to play around with their mother's necklace or chain.

## Contraceptive effects of Breastfeeding

Breastfeeding is more likely to have a contraceptive effect if the mother is breastfeeding exclusively through the day and night. That is, she is not giving the baby any other milk or water.

When the mother breastfeeds in this way, she is also likely not to have a menstrual period.

Both of the above are likely to be the case within the first 6 months of the child's life. Therefore, if a mother is exclusively breastfeeding a baby less than 6 months of age, and not having a period, her chances of becoming pregnant are as low as 2%. Each time she feeds the baby she releases prolactin, a hormone that suppresses ovulation.

## Breast or Bottle

The advantages or breastfeeding undoubtedly far outweigh bottle-feeding. Sometimes the bottle may be resorted to for some reason. There is no need to feel guilty if that is the case. The aim of both is a well–nourished, happy and active baby.

At times bottle–feeding may be resorted to if the mother is working. In that case the baby can still take one or two breastfeeds, early morning and late at night.

If the baby does not gain adequate weight bottle-feeding is often resorted to. However, the mother should also be reminded that the hindmilk or the last part of the breast milk is rich in fat. If the initial watery milk is 20% fat, the hindmilk is 50% fat. Babies who are fed the hindmilk sleep well and grow healthy. The fat content increases gradually towards the end of the feed. If the mother feeds from one breast at one feed for 20 to 30 minutes, the baby is likely to get the fat rich hindmilk.

At times recurrent cracking of nipples, mastitis, or surgery for the mother might lead to a switch.

An exhausted mother, unable to cope with demand feeding and other household chores, may get so tired and anxious that it might interfere with her lactation. It is therefore advisable to arrange for extra help at this time.

*Calorie Content of Breast Milk*

Foremilk  1.5 cal/ounce

Hindmilk  25–30 cal/ounce

*Source: Dr. Richard Applebaum,* Nursing your Baby,

A woman may have in-laws, friends, or a husband who are not very enthusiastic about breastfeeding. On the other hand, some women may give up breastfeeding from wrong advice or hearsay, for example, some women believe breastfeeding ruins their figures. There is no credibility in this, as it has been seen from medical experience that many women breastfeed several babies with no bad effects on their figure. Others end up with even better figures. Very few women give up breastfeeding for the reasons listed above. Basically if a woman decides to breastfeed, she normally succeeds. Most mothers give up because they feel they have fed long enough or as long as they had planned.

A breastfed baby is not prone to allergies. There are less chances of diarrhoea, eczema, coughs, colds, and asthma in breastfed babies.

Some women fear feeding will make them less sexy. This is not true, since sex, childbirth and breastfeeding are linked with the same hormone. Many women feel more sexy when feeding.

It is easier to breastfeed if you are travelling. No hassles of sterilising bottles and running around to find a place to make feeds. All you need is yourself and maybe a shawl or scarf to cover yourself discreetly.

## How Long to Breastfeed?

A working mother can combine breastfeeding with bottle-feeding. Ideally a baby should be breastfed for 2 years; or, for a minimum of 6 months.

Some mothers feed for 1 year or 8 months. The reason why breastfeeding is recommended for 2 years is that it gives the baby greater immunity to fight infection during the teething phase. At that time the baby will also be eating other food, and breastfeeding maybe done just once or twice a day. Also, if the mother is an air hostess or a doctor, her duty hours could be 24 hours or longer, so that the bottle will have to be resorted to.

## Breastfeeding and the Working Woman

If you know you have to go back to work, it is wise to combine breastfeeding and bottle-feeding. At the start give the baby a breastfeed whenever it demands a feed, except for one bottle-feed in the morning around 10 a.m. When the baby is 2 months old, start introducing a routine, in which you gradually cut out breastfeeds and introduce bottle-feeds instead.

*Breast to bottle*

Start by cutting out breastfeeds that are due at the time you are likely to be away to work. By the 3rd month you can be giving 3 to 4 breastfeeds, 1 early in the morning and 2 in the evenings. Or, 2 in the mornings and 2 in the evenings. You can also introduce mashed bananas (slightly overripe) and bland preparations of *khichdi / kheer / halwa / upma/* any *daal* without *tarka* with little *ghee* / mashed potato.

If your work is going to require you to be away for a few days on and off, switch to the bottle totally by the 3rd month.

> ### Quickies
>
> In order to reduce preparation time before a feed, or to be able to carry a quickie food while travelling, the following ready mix powder can be kept handy. Take some rice grains and roast them on the *tava* or in a cooking vessel over the fire. When roasted cool them and dry— grind them in a mixie, so that you get ready cooked rice powder. Bottle it. When required you can add water, milk, watery *dal* or any other liquid to it and feed the baby. You could do the same with other grains like wheat grains or *ragi*.

If you want to increase the number of breastfeeds and reduce the number of bottle-feeds, breastfeeding more

*Bottle to breastfeed*

209

often will cause the release of prolactin hormone and an increase in breast milk production.

Each time you are to give a bottle-feed, first put the baby to the breast, and then give the other milk with a spoon, not from the bottle. Gradually, in a few days your own milk supply will build up and you will not need the other milk at all.

## Case Against the Bottle

Bottle-feeding should be resorted to when absolutely necessary, and its potential hazards must be borne in mind. Bottle-feeding also requires a lot of hard work, since one has to sterilise the feeding bottles, nipples, etc., and make the feeds. This is very important. If sterilising is not done properly, it can cause diarrhoea and dehydration in the baby. If the milk is not made properly, it can mean a sick baby.

Once you start on bottle-feed, the baby may begin to prefer it. It will upset the balance of your milk supply, which will be reduced.

The contraceptive effect of breastfeeding will also lessen.

If you give a bottle-feed at night you will have to be fully alert and awake to make a bottle-feed and bring it to the right temperature. It is easier to simply put the baby to the breast.

## The Bottle and Nipple confusion

Feeding the baby from the bottle causes nipple confusion, and should be avoided. At the breast the baby needs to work hard with its jaw to feed. The bottle on the other hand drips milk regardless of the baby's jaw effort. The baby gets used to this easy flow from the bottle's nipple and dislikes working hard at the breast's nipple.

The disadvantage of the constant flow of the bottle's nipple is that the baby needs to suck and swallow quickly. This results in a respiratory load on the child and is not recommended at all for small babies or premature babies. It would be similar to your being asked to finish a bottle of water or cola without a break. It would leave you gasping for breath.

Further, the baby gets used to overfeeding when drinking from the bottle. This can sow the seeds of overeating and obesity.

## Milk Powder

Making a powdered-milk feed should be done exactly according to the instructions on the can. Some people put extra milk powder in the feed, since they feel the milk looks very thin. This could be dangerous. It could lead to a concentration of minerals in the baby's bloodstream, which can lead to dehydration and illness.

On the other hand, some people might put less milk powder as compared to the instructions on the can, thus running into the danger of giving inadequate nourishment to the baby.

You must discuss with your doctor which is the best milk to give the baby. If you are going to be travelling a lot, it is best to give powdered milk, so that there are less frequent changes, since you can carry the milk powder with you wherever you go. Besides, it is sterilised and does not become easily infected. The brand you use should not be changed; it is best to stick to one brand.

When making a feed, a little extra milk can be prepared, in case the baby wants to have a little extra.

If it is not consumed, the extra milk should be thrown away after a feed.

Milk can be made in a large jug and kept covered in the refrigerator for not more than 24 hours. Little quantities of it can be transferred to sterilised bottles when needed. Or, milk can be poured in sterilised bottles and kept in the refrigerator. When needed, it can be removed, warmed, by using a bottle warmer or a mug of hot water, before use. It is a good rule to follow, rather than let someone else make the milk.

## Cow's Milk

Cow's milk has more protein than mother's milk. This unnaturally large intake of protein results in an large load of nitrogen for the infant's kidneys. Cow's milk should therefore be given diluted with one part water to three parts of cow's milk. The water dilutes the protein and minerals like sodium and nitrogen.

A little sugar should be added to the milk, since mother's milk has more lactose than cow's milk.

## How to Sterilise Bottles

You must keep aside a large vessel in the kitchen for boiling bottles in. You can buy one with a lid, since a covered vessel uses up less fuel. You will also need a bottle brush, which you must make sure is kept clean.

Unscrew the covers of the bottles. Separate nipples. In order to get the slime off the nipples, rinse them in water, then apply salt inside and outside them and put them in the sun on a plate.

Wash the bottles, rims and covers of the bottles,

use a liquid soap like Teepol or a soapy solution of Surf detergent power. Scrub them well with the brush to remove the slime that milk tends to leave behind. If left behind, the slime forms a breeding ground for germs. You could fill used bottles with water after use so that milk does not dry in them and they are easier to clean. When the bottles are nicely scrubbed clean, fill them with water before you immerse them in the vessel of water, so that you have a minimum number of air bubbles in the bottles and they remain nicely submerged.

When all parts of the bottle are scrubbed and immersed in water, put the vessel on fire, with its lid on it. When the water boils, it will send up steam and bubbles of air, and make a gurgling sound. It is important that this stage is reached, for only when the water boils actively do the germs get killed.

When the water is boiling, bring the nipples inside and wash them thoroughly in running water, to remove every trace of salt. It should not be left behind in the nipple, since the baby should not get an unnecessary extra daily dosage of salt. Then remove the lid of the vessel, put the nipples in the vessel and turn off the flame after a couple of minutes.

When the water is cool enough to handle, wash your hands with soap and remove the feeding equipment. Fix the nipples on the rims, and put the covers on the bottles and keep aside for use during the day.

213

If you have to go out to work, you can make the milk and pour it into individual covered or sealed bottles and leave behind in the refrigerator, so that it can be fed while you are away.

## How to Bottle-feed

The baby, while being bottle-fed, should be held close as in breastfeeding. Do not place the baby on the bed and feed it like a doll. Bottle-feeding should not only provide nourishment, but also warmth and security to the child. You can also hold the baby next to your naked skin. This is specially important if the baby has been separated from you earlier on, on account of illness, premature birth or any other reason. The mutual feedback you and your baby get from each other at this time will build a new relationship and bond between you both.

Before giving the bottle, check the temperature of the milk by letting a few drops of milk fall on the back of your hand from the bottle. If the milk feels pleasantly warm, it is the right temperature. If it feels hot, cool it by waiting a little or placing it in cold water. If the milk is made and kept in the refrigerator in sterilised bottles, there is no harm in giving the baby cold milk. If it is winter and the milk from the fridge is too cold, it can be stood in a mug of hot water before being fed to the baby.

If during a feed you have to keep the bottle aside for a little while, cover it with a special cap that comes with feeding bottles. Do not let the nipple be exposed to flies or do not cover it with your hanky or towel. Avoid touching the nipple with the fingers.

When feeding, hold the baby upright, that is, head

214

higher than the rest of the body. Hold the bottle firmly at a slant, and make sure the nipple reaches way back in the baby's mouth. The nipple should always be full of milk, or else the baby will take in too much air and have a lot of wind. If the teat flattens and the milk stops going through, pull the bottle gently backwards to release the vacuum.

Check if the nipple's hole is large enough. When the bottle is inverted, it should allow several drops to flow in one second. If you find the flow is very slow, enlarge the hole with a red hot needle. Hold the tip of the needle in a flame, and when it becomes red hot in colour with the heat, pierce the tip of the nipple with it.

Let the baby have a pause during a feed, now and then. Burp the baby.

## Problems during Breastfeeding

If a mother has too much milk that flows too fast, the baby might choke on it. In case this happens, the mother should express a little milk before feeding the baby.

*When the baby chokes*

Sometimes the baby may choke if the mother's nipples are too big and long, so that they go past the hard palate and touch the soft palate. The baby turns its head away from the breast and cries, moving his arms and legs. In this case, the mother should hold the baby a little away from the breast.

When you want to stop feeding, if you pull and drag the baby off the breast, it might give you sore nipples. So instead, you must break the baby's suction by putting the tip of your finger in the corner of the mouth between the gums, and then take him/her off the breast.

*Sore nipples*

215

### Feeding Bra

A feeding bra should be worn, so that the breasts do not sag with the extra weight. Due to the extra weight of the breasts, the bra should be well fitted and made of cotton, since cotton does not stretch with the increase in size, and therefore gives better support. It also allows better absorbency and circulation of air, hence reducing chances of sore nipples. During pregnancy, if the bra fits well but is tight below the breast, you can buy some extra bra hooks called extension and fix at the back, to make the bra more comfortable.

The bra should not be too tight. It should not have bands at the top of the breasts, that cut into the skin when the front cup or flap opens for feeding. This can cause blocked ducts. You can remove the bra at night.

Or, pull the chin of the baby downwards.

If you press your breast down with the finger, by forming a big dent on the breast, in order to prevent the baby's nose from getting blocked, the act of pressing the breast down will cause the nipple to project upwards and hit the roof of the baby's mouth when it feeds. This hitting of the nipple on the hard palate will cause it to get sore. Besides it will block release of milk from the front tip of the nipple.

Soreness sometimes occurs if the nipples are frequently washed with soap. Water is sufficient to wash them with. Pressure applied at the same point constantly can also lead to soreness. It therefore helps to change positions during a feed and to adopt different positions for different feeds, so that pressure is applied to different points on the breast.

Soreness may be caused by a baby sucking too long after the breast has been emptied. A baby takes approximately 20 minutes to empty a breast; after that he/she only indulges in comfort sucking. Restrict comfort sucking.

### How to Heal Sore Nipples

Soggy nipples, that is, nipples that remain wet for long periods, are more prone to soreness. It therefore helps to expose your nipples to air and sunlight as much as possible, until the soreness heals. You can wear a loose garment without a bra, or you can wear a tea–strainer without a handle inside your bra, to promote healing.

> **Home Remedy**
>
> You could dab the sore area with cotton soaked in water to which a few drops of calendula Q, a homoeopathic medicine has been added, and leave it to dry.

Avoid using creams on cracked nipples. Dry cornflour can be dusted on them instead. It is also very helpful to express some milk after a feed and rub it on the sore nipple where it should be left to dry. This quickens healing considerably. Avoid the use of water proof backed bra pads. Do not remove any crust appearing on the nipple. It is part of the healing process.

Always offer the less sore side first. That will establish the flow on the sore side before the baby takes it, thus making it less painful. You can use breathing for labour to be able to handle the pain. An aspirin or a mild alcoholic drink (beer or wine) taken shortly before a feed will help reduce the pain. It can be taken if the pain begins to interfere with the let down or release of milk.

You can try using a cold compress on your nipples before feeding. Apply an ice cube wrapped in a towel or hanky. You can wear a blotting paper or an ever dry nappy liner inside the bra to keep the nipples dry. Sometimes, a sore nipple may bleed. There is no harm if the baby swallows tiny amounts of blood with the milk. This can be quite frightening, especially when the baby burps after a feed, and along with the curdled milk brings up a little blood. However, this is harmless to the baby.

**Home Remedy**

The last part of expressed breast milk applied on the sore nipple will encourage it to heal.

Continue to treat your sore nipples and carry on feeding.

There may be a risk of infection of sore nipples, if the baby has thrush, that is, white spots on the tongue that do not wipe away. Thrush must be treated medically. You can take the baby off the breast for a few feeds until the skin has healed. The milk can be expressed and fed to the baby from a spoon. Gentain violet can be applied to the baby's tongue to clear it of the thrush.

A nipple shield can be used. It is a rubber shield that fits over the nipple and areola and prevents direct suction on the nipple.

*Blocked ducts*

A blocked duct appears in the form of a tender red-looking lump on the breast or areola. It feels sore and can be accompanied by a hot and shivery feeling.

It can be caused from pressure on the breast, as from a tight bra. Or, you may be holding the baby too tightly against the breast, or your arm may be pressing on the side of the breast when lying in an uncomfortable position.

It can also be caused during engorgement by inadequate emptying of one duct in particular. This, or any of the above factors, can cause a milk duct to get blocked, so that it does not empty properly, causing a tender or painful lump to appear.

### How to Deal with a Blocked Duct

Gentle but firm massage of the lump towards the nipple during a feed and after, if the block is still there, will help. A hot water bottle should ease the pain; also a hot wet compress applied hourly. Do not stop feeding. Offer the affected breast first for a few feeds, to ensure vigorous sucking, and drainage of the blocked duct. Lean forward over the baby as you feed, so that gravity also operates. Give the baby some extra feeds. Express the remaining milk after a feed.

Check for tight bras, specially if your bra has a band across the top of the breast, when the flap is open.

Get plenty of rest. Actually go to bed for a day, it will make you feel better and make sure the blocked duct does not lead to mastitis.

Exercise of the arms, shoulders, and upper half of the body may help disperse the painful swelling caused by a blocked duct.

The symptoms are similar to those of a blocked duct. The infected area is red, swollen, hot and painful, with shiny skin. The mother may feel nausea and shivering, as in flu.

*Non-infective mastitis*

It may be caused by milk leaking from a blocked duct into the surrounding tissues and bloodstream. The treatment for this is the same as the treatment for blocked ducts, with the addition of an antibiotic.

There is no danger in continuing feeding, as the organisms responsible for this sort of breast infection are not harmful and rarely present in breast milk.

This sort of sporadic mastitis often occurs after several weeks of feeding and occasionally without a duct being blocked.

It normally occurs in the first 2 weeks of feeding. Its symptoms are that the whole breast is red, hot, tender and swollen, and the mother feels feverish and ill. The milk becomes infected by a germ carried in the baby's nose from the hospital nursery. The infection involves

*Infective mastitis*

219

the milk duct.

It the milk is infected, the baby may have to be taken off the affected breast temporarily. The baby can be fed from the non infected breast or be given powdered milk, or cow's milk. The breast should be emptied regularly and the milk discarded until the bacteria count in the milk comes down to safe limits.

In the meantime, take rest and plenty of fluids. Also, swinging your arms (bent at the elbows) backward and forward will help.

*Prevention of mastitis*

To avoid mastitis, the lactating mother should check her breasts for blocked ducts daily. The examination should preferably be done when the breasts are relatively soft and empty. They should be checked for red patches. Fingers can be lightly swept over the breasts to check for any unusual hardness which will be different from the all over hardness of a breast full of milk.

The appearance of a red patch or lumpy hardness in the breasts means that a woman is heading for a blocked duct. The moment signs of a blocked duct are noticed, the baby should be allowed to suck at that breast as soon as possible. While the baby is feeding, massaging the lump towards the nipple helps to unblock the duct.

To prevent blocked ducts and engorgement, keep the breasts well drained. This can be done by feeding the baby regularly and frequently, and by expressing any surplus milk that makes the breast uncomfortable. It can be done with your hands, or with the aid of a breast pump.

Sometimes, the mother becoming cold probably leads to blocked ducts, because it causes circulatory changes in the breasts, or because of the change in temperature that it causes in the mammary gland, it changes its bacterial environment. Hence mothers who are feeding should be comfortably warm and not take long swims.

Failure to treat mastitis or unnecessary weaning following mastitis may lead to breast abscess. A woman must not stop feeding or expressing milk when she gets mastitis. The lump of a breast abscess is hard, red and painful.

*Breast*
*abscess*

It requires treatment by antibiotics or surgical drainage. The baby may have to be taken off the affected breast. He can feed from the other breast until treatment is completed.

If a breast abscess is accompanied by a sore nipple, a nipple shield may be recommended by your doctor. The nipple shield fits over the nipple, and prevents direct force on the nipple. However, if the breast abscess is near the nipple, and the nipple shield also covers the abscess when worn, it can be very painful. Therefore, avoid a nipple shield if the abscess is too close to the nipple.

The milk from the affected breast may be temporarily expressed and discarded. However, if the doctor feels that infection from the abscess is not present in the milk, he may not advise you to take the baby off the breast.

## Babies with Problems

If the baby is put in an incubator for special care immediately after birth, and it is not allowed to come to you for feeds, express or pump your colostrum. It can be fed to the baby by a nurse with the help of a

*Feeding*
*in the*
*incubator*

spoon, dropper, tube, or drops fed from a soaked gauze. Do not be dismayed if the amount of colostrum seems very little. Remember it is very little in the beginning, but each drop of it is worth its weight in gold, when you consider all the advantages it is going to give your baby.

Subsequently breast milk should be expressed and fed to the baby in the incubator. Or, better still, the mother can go to the nursery to suckle the baby at feed time.

*Jaundice*                There are three kinds of jaundice :

| Kind of Jaundice | When it Occurs |
| --- | --- |
| Physiological jaundice | Occurs on the 2nd or 4th day and lasts for about a week. |
| Abnormal jaundice | Occurs within the first 24 hours after birth. |
| Breast milk jaundice | Starts at the end of the 1st week of life. Worst during 2nd and 3rd weeks. Can last up to 2 months. |

## Physiological Jaundice

Physiological jaundice is fairly common, mild, and usually harmless. Within the uterus the baby has an abundance of red blood cells. Once the baby is born and breathing, excessive amount of red blood cells is not needed, so they break down until the level of cells is appropriate for the baby. A by-product of the breakdown is bilirubin, which deposits in the skin and white of the eye, evident as yellow colouring.

Physiological jaundice normally appears after

222

er
Breastfeeding

30 hours. Peak levels of bilirubin are reached on the 4th or 5th day, and eyes return to their normal colour by the 7th day. In physiological jaundice the bilirubin level normally does not exceed 10 mg/100 ml.

## Abnormal Jaundice

This kind of jaundice is today a thing of the past. An early pregnancy blood test identifies women with blood group incompatibility *(see p.60)*. Such women are given an Anti D immunoglobulin injection to prevent abnormal jaundice in the child. When this injection is not given, it results in blood group incompatibility.

That is, jaundice that occurs in the first 24 hours. It is more severe and serious and is called haemolytic jaundice. It may be the result of blood group incompatibility between the mother and the baby and needs urgent treatment to prevent brain damage in the child. The baby needs to be treated in a hospital. It may require complete transfusion of blood, after which breastfeeding can continue normally.

It is quite safe to feed your baby even if your blood group is rhesus negative and your baby's is rhesus positive. Rhesus antibodies are present in breast milk if they are present in the mother's blood, but they get inactivated by digestion in the baby's gut; therefore you can safely feed the baby. It is also quite safe to breastfeed after having an injection of Anti-D immunoglobulin.

## Breast Milk Jaundice

This is a rare kind of jaundice that develops about 1 week after birth and could continue for 2 months.

### When Not to Breastfeed

Mothers suffering from tuberculosis, chronic nephritis (kidney trouble), or severe psychiatric disorders will be asked not to breastfeed; also mothers who have suffered from some malignant disease. Some patients of epilepsy may be discouraged from feeding if they are on a drug that can be excreted in breast milk.

Although the jaundice can become as deep as 20 mg bilirubin per 100 ml of serum it does not harm the baby's brain, because it occurs after the first week of life, when the blood brain barrier is reasonably well developed. You can continue breastfeeding.

However, if your baby's bilirubin level rises too high, your paediatrician may request you to interrupt breastfeeding for a short while, say, 6 to 12 hours. If at the end of this time the bilirubin level has fallen by more than, say, 2 mg per 100 ml of serum, breastfeeding can be resumed. Usually the bilirubin level then rises slightly before falling slowly and steadily. If the level rises during the break or breaks, the jaundice is not being caused by breast milk, and other causes will need to be investigated.

Other causes of prolonged jaundice could be infection, metabolic conditions such as low blood sugar, or even administration of drugs to the mother in pregnancy.

While your baby is off breast milk, keep your milk supply going by expression or pumping more frequently than your baby would have fed, and discard your milk until your milk can again be fed.

Generally jaundice is no cause to stop breastfeeding. Some people wrongly believe that breast milk jaundice means that breastfeeding should completely stop. This is not so. The condition resolves itself spontaneously in time with no ill effects on the baby from breast milk.

## Treatment

Babies with moderately raised levels of bilirubin are often treated by being placed uncovered in a cot 16 inches beneath a daylight fluorescent tube with their eyes covered. This is called phototherapy. There is no harm if you take the baby from under the light every 2 hours to feed, and may be more often if she demands it. Remove the eye covers when you feed.

If your baby is otherwise well, your paediatrician may agree to your taking your baby home and giving it exposure to sunlight. You can place the baby naked next to the window, but make sure she/he does not get too hot or too cold. You can blindfold the baby if the sunlight is too strong, so that it does not affect the baby's eyesight. You may have to take your baby back to the hospital for blood tests.

### Phototherapy

To treat high bilirubin levels the baby may be exposed to contolled amounts of ultra-violet light, which breaks down the pigment levels in the skin. The shades protect the baby from the light.

# Cleft Palate

A cleft palate means that there is an opening on the roof of the baby's mouth. It might sometimes be accompanied by a cleft in the lip also. The cause of the cleft happens sometime within the first 3 months of the baby's development in the womb. There is not much you could have done about it, so do not add to your anxiety with your worry. Besides, do not let your relationship with your partner be tinged with unnecessary suspicion that the anomaly was caused by the other. Accept the baby and love it. Do not blame yourself.

A baby with a cleft lip and palate cannot suck. However, it can cup feed with considerable ease (*see p.198*). For such a baby, cup feeding has the added advantage of making the muscles of its upper lip work.

Feeding a baby with a cleft palate can be difficult. The baby needs to attach itself properly to the breast so that it can suck well. The best position at the breast for a baby with a cleft palate is one with the nose and throat higher than the breast. The upright position is therefore very good.

The baby's body should be in an upright position close to the mother's. This position will prevent milk from leaking through the opening on the roof of the baby's mouth into the nose. If milk does go into the baby's nose, it makes it difficult for the baby to breathe. When the baby is well attached to the breast, the breast tissue closes over the cleft and helps the baby suck well.

Babies with a cleft palate have a tendency for their tongue to fall back. So another good position for feeding such a baby is with the mother lying on her back and the baby lying on top of her for feeding. This position ensures that the baby's tongue remains forward thus making it possible for the baby to suck well.

Apart from the above positions, the mother can also express milk and feed it with a spoon to the baby placed on her lap with the head held higher than the rest of the body.

The baby will have to be fed thus until the condition can be rectified by surgery. Generally 2 or 3 surgeries will be required. Apart from the paediatrician, the parents will also have to consult a plastic surgeon, a dentist, a prosthodontist, and maybe a speech therapist.

As suggested by a leading paediatrician, a dentist (prosthodontist) may be consulted to fit the baby with an artificial palate to cover the gap on the roof of the baby's mouth, so that the baby can be breastfed. Some doctors fear that the artificial palate might cause infection at the site. But with breast milk the baby will receive infection fighting properties and put on weight. Besides, any wound arising from the procedure will heal really quickly in a day or two, since it is in the mouth, an area where healing is quick.

Whether the mother nurses the baby at the breast, or with a spoon, she should cuddle the baby and keep trying to nurse it at the breast. Such non-nutritive suckling helps mother and baby bond to each other.

A cleft palate and/or lip must be operated within a year, before the baby starts to speak. Sometimes a baby with a cleft palate may be more prone to ear infections.

This condition requires an enormous amount of patience on the part of the parents. However, one day, all of your efforts will be behind you and your baby's condition will stand corrected with no cosmetic and functional problem. At the present moment, if your baby does have this problem, it will help immensely if you can be in touch with a couple who has gone through a similar experience recently. It may be someone distantly related or an acquaintance. Search them out for they can be beacons of moral support to you. If you do not know anyone, or meet someone who is not forthcoming, ask your paediatrician or plastic surgeon.

# 16. Conditions that May Require Surgery at Birth

When the baby is born there is a lot of excitement and a sigh of relief at the birth. The mother is tired but happy. The baby is looked at by the attending doctor, and now in most major centres and hospitals the delivery is attended by a paediatrician who examines the baby for normal reflexes and that the baby is breathing normally and has no obvious congenital anomalies.

It is increasingly becoming common to have antenatally diagnosed surgical conditions of which the parents are already aware of. When such a situation arises then it is imperative that the parents are in touch with a paediatric surgeon so as to counsel them about the problem. This is important as often the problem is completely curable and rarely is it life threatening. Either way, it is good for the family to be mentally prepared.

There are a few conditions that alert the doctor to the immediate need for surgery in the baby:

| | |
|---|---|
| *Gastroschisis* | The intestines are lying outside the abdomen through an opening in the abdomen. |
| *Omphalocoel* | A sac is covering the extruded intestines. |
| *Oesophageal Atresia & Tracheo-Oesophageal Fistula* | The baby has increased frothing at the mouth and is unable to accept feeds, due to a communication between the air pipe (trachea) and food pipe (oesophagus). |
| *Diaphragmatic Hernia* | The baby has breathing difficulty. The abdomen is flattened and the intestines and liver are lying in the chest and are detected clinically by hearing bowel sounds in the chest and plain X-ray of the chest reveals bowel shadows in the chest. |

| | |
|---|---|
| *Imperforate anus* | There is no anal opening. |

## Other conditions needing immediate surgery are:

| | |
|---|---|
| The baby vomits and does not pass stool and develops abdominal distention, that is, the tummy becomes big. | *Intestinal Atresia* |
| It may manifest itself in vomiting and delayed passage of meconium, that is, the dark brown or black stool passed by the baby at birth. | *Hirschsprung's disease* |

## Some conditions are present at birth, but require planned surgery, that is, there is no need to do emergency surgery :

| | |
|---|---|
| Often waiting and watching a while will allow the hernia effect to close spontaneously. | *Umbilical Hernia* |
| The urethral opening is on the underside (ventral aspect ) of the penis and the penis is curved. | *Hypospadias* |
| The urethral opening is on the  upper side (dorsal aspect ) of the penis and the penis appears short. | *Epispadias* |
| The bladder and the urethra are open. | *Extrophy Bladder* |
| These are best operated at about 2 to 3 months.  Hydroceles often resolve themselves by waiting on them.  Undescended testes, if they do not come down to the scrotum by one year, require surgical intervention. | *Hernia Hydrocele, Inguinal Hernias Undescended Testes* |
| Another problem that is perplexing is Ambiguous Genitalia, boy or girl? The parents are anxious and sometimes even doctors do not | *Ambiguous Genitalia* |

229

have an immediate answer. It is helpful to have the history of the mother: If she has had some androgenic hormones during pregnancy, or if there are other female children who have a large phallus. The latter suggests a diagnosis of congenital adrenal hyperplasia – a condition in girls who have an enlarged clitoris. Specialised X-rays help us to diagnose a male who has undescended testes and has a small phallus.

Sometimes the baby is truly intersex and with the help of hormonal and chromosomal studies we can designate and make the baby a male or a female according to circumstances. The patient should be assessed by a paediatrician and a paediatric surgeon, to discuss the further course of action.

Dr. Meera Luthra
M.S., M.Ch. DNB (Paediatric Surgery)
Senior Consultant Surgeon
Apollo Indraprastha Hospital, New Delhi

# 17. Teratogenesis

Teratogenesis means the formation of abnormalities in the baby during intrauterine life. The factors that lead to formation of these abnormalities are known as teratogens. Such abnormalities may be obvious when the baby is born or may remain undetected for a long time after birth. The degree of such abnormalities, if present, depends upon a large number of factors, to name a few, the genetic make-up of the baby, the period of gestation (pregnancy), the maternal health at the time of exposure to the teratogen, and the intensity and duration of exposure of the mother to the teratogen.

Factors which lead to teratogenesis are as follows:

---

*Infections*  Infections in the mother, like viral infections, bacterial infections and a few fungal infections. Any micro-organisms or the toxins released by them, which cross the placenta and reach the baby, might interfere with the growth and development of the baby, thereby leading to malformations in the baby.

---

*Addictions*  Drugs, liquor, smoking and other addictions like tobacco chewing etc. in the mother. These cross the placental barrier and might damage the baby. If the damage is too intense, it might lead to abortion. If the damage is of a lesser intensity, the baby is born as an addict, to any of these agents.

---

■ Long-term antibiotics, anti-psychotic drugs like anti-depressants, mood elevators, sleeping pills, etc.   *Chemical factors*

■ Drugs used for cancer treatment and hormones given as a therapeutic measure will have teratogenic effect if the woman happens to be pregnant during such treatment. Such pregnancies might be terminated to save the life of the mother.

---

231

*Physical agents*

- Lowering of oxygen pressure in the blood of the mother during flights. This is unlikely to happen in modern aircrafts, unless there is a fall in cabin pressure, in which case the mother-to-be should grasp the oxygen mask and breathe deeply. Also she should avoid visits to high altitude areas like Leh and Ladakh, for the same reason.

- Exposure to X-rays, physical violence, trauma, radiation from sources like atom bombs, solar eclipse, etc., can turn out to be harmful for both mother and baby. Physical trauma can occur from rough journeys, sports like horse riding, trekking, mountaineering, or gymnastics undertaken during sexual activities.

| | |
|---|---|
| *Industrial pollution* | This is relevant for women employed in various industries. Casual exposure to pollution is not likely to have noticeable effects. |
| *Malnutrition* | Vitamin and mineral deficiencies can cause inadequate or under development of the baby. |

It is very important for every pregnant woman to realise that she should protect herself from all such factors, which might lead to fetal abnormalities, especially if she is exposed to these factors during the first 4 months of pregnancy.

These factors might either affect the placenta or, if they cross the placental barrier and reach the baby, will interfere with its growth and development.

## Precautions to be taken during pregnancy

- Relax mentally and physically, so that you do not need any medicines to keep you calm. Over-exhaustion can cause sleeplessness. Short periods of rest twice or thrice during the day are recommended.

- Take a balanced diet. The golden rule about diet is, 'Eat a little bit of every food item but excess of nothing.' If necessary consult your doctor for supplementation of vitamins, iron, calcium, etc. Some women get morning sickness or vomit a lot or do not feel like eating. These women should avoid foods which lead to gastric irritation and they should eat small quantities of nourishing food more frequently during the afternoons or evenings when the nausea is relatively less.

- Nowadays, young women want to maintain their slim figures. Some women think that if they eat less, their babies will be smaller and they will have an easier delivery. The fetus is like a parasite and it will draw all the nutrition it needs whether the mother has enough or not. This results in malnourishment of the mother. It is advisable that the mother takes adequate quantity of a well-balanced diet.

- Avoid consuming liquor, tobacco or any habit-forming drugs. It is wise to avoid the company of addicts. This will keep you away from temptation and social pressures to consume such items. Spending time in the company of smokers leads to passive smoking on the part of the mother.

- Protect yourself from all kinds of infections. Do not visit sick relatives or friends. Send a bouquet of flowers or a 'get well' card instead. Avoid visits to hospitals as you are likely to be exposed to a large number of infections. Avoid going to crowded places like cinema halls, markets, etc.

- Protect yourself from physical agents like fatigue, exhaustion, jerky journeys, joy rides in amusement parks, horse riding, etc.

- Avoid taking medicines altogether, if you can. If you get a headache or a backache use a pain balm instead of painkillers.

- Avoid being X-rayed. Tell your doctor about your pregnancy.

---

Do not be over anxious about teratogenesis; otherwise your mental tension will create problems for you. Take time off to relax mentally and physically. Remember, 50% of your baby's health depends upon hereditary factors and the other 50%

depends upon how well you look after yourself.

During this period, members of your family tend to pamper you. Make the most of it and allow yourself to be looked after by them. This is their way of looking after you and your baby. If you feel that they are not giving you enough attention, then do not get into spells of depression. Instead, go out of your way and look after yourself, and the baby will be looked after automatically by you.

Dr. Asha Singh

MBBS, MS, Ph. D (Genetics),
Prof. of Anatomy,
Maulana Azad Medical College, New Delhi

# Recommended Reading

## Pregnancy and Birth along with Practical Tips

**Pregnancy and Childbirth**
*Sheila Kitzinger*
Michael Joseph Ltd, 1980.

**The Encyclopaedia of Pregnancy and Birth**
*Janet Balaskas, Yehudi Gordon*
MacDonald & Co. Ltd, 1989.

**New Active Birth** *Janet Balaskas*
Unwin Paperbacks,1989.

## A New Look at Birth, stressing on the calm and quiet aspects of Birth

**Birth without Violence**
*Dr. Frederick Leboyer*
Fontana / Collins, 1977.

**Birth Reborn**
*Dr. Michel Odent*
Fontana / Collins, 1986.

## Breastfeeding

**The Breastfeeding Book**
*Marie Messenger Davis*
Century Hutchinson Ltd., 1988.

**Helping Mothers to Breastfeed,**
*Felicity Savage and R.K. Anand. 1992*
*Available from:* Association for Consumer
Action on Safety and Health (ACASH)
P.O.Box 2498, Mumbai 400 002

**Breast Feeding, the Best Option** *1994*
*Available from:* Survival for Women &
Children Foundation (SWACH)
Sector 16, Panchkula, Haryana 134 113
Tel (0172) 267770, 278376

## Childcare

**Dr. R.K.Anand's Guide to Childcare**
*Dr.R.K. Anand*
Vakils, Feffer & Simons Ltd, 2001.

**Baby and Child Care** *Dr.R.K.Suneja*
Rupa & Co, 1998.
This includes addresses of:
• Institutions for the Handicapped
• Thallesemics India
• Main Center for Genetic Studies

**What do You Really Want From Your Children?**
*Dr. Wayne W. Dyer*
Arrow Books, 1997.

*Miscellaneous*

**Woman's Experience of Sex**
*Sheila Kitzinger*
G.P. Putnam's Sons, 1983.
A comprehensive book on sexual behaviour,
feelings, difficulties, phases, grieving etc:

**Hum Kya Khaiyen?**
**(What Should We eat?)** *Dr. Ramesh Bijlani*
NCERT, 1989.
A book in Hindi that deals with Indian conditions,
and answers questions regarding a balanced diet,
*ghee*, cholesterol, constipation, illness, etc.

**Magical Child** *J.C.Pearce*
Bantam Books, New York, 1986.
Highly recommended serious reading on how to
positively influence a child from birth onwards,
and infant and child rearing from a different but
scientific perspective.

**Child Development** *Elizabeth B. Hurlock*
McGraw Hill Co., (Psychology Series), 1978.
An excellent book on psychological, physical,
social, emotional, moral and all-round
development of a child.

**Touch me, Touch-me-not,** *1997*
*Available from:* Kali for Women
B1/8, Hauz Khas, New Delhi 110 016
A book on the use of common Indian plants for
healing of women's diseases like vaginal
discharge, urinary tract infections, menstrual
disorders, uterine complaints etc.

# Informed Choices

*WHO Recommendations (Source Laucet (AQ:) 1985, 2:437)*

The World Health Organisation (WHO) recognises the importance of natural childbirth, and recommends that minimum technology be used in childbirth. In 1985, WHO held a conference on appropriate technlogy for birth. Over 50 participants specialising in obstetrics, paediatrics and other relevant professions came toghether in Fortaleza, Brazil. The participants unanimously adopted recommendations which WHO believes are relevant to the entire world. (Lancet 1985 2:437)

WHO Recommends:

*IT IS NOT RECOMMENDED THAT PREGNANT WOMEN BE PLACED IN A DORSAL LITHOTOMY POSITION DURING LABOUR AND DELIVERY. WALKING SHOULD BE ENCOURAGED DURING LABOUR AND EACH WOMAN MUST FREELY DECIDE WHICH POSITION TO ADOPT DURING DELIVERY.*

In simple words what this means, is that women in labour should be allowed to adopt upright positions like walking, standing, sitting, kneeling etc., rather than being made to lie down flat on their backs. Indeed, in labour, when a woman lies flat on her back, it is of disadvantage to her because of the following reasons.

Firstly, it results in the compression of a major blood vessel called the Vena Cava, which is positioned between the pregnant uterus and the mother's backbone. Compression of this blood vessel reduces the flow of blood to and from the heart, thus reducing the amount of oxygen available in the mother's body, to be used by both, the mother and the bady. Therefore if the mother does not lie flat on her back, the amount of oxygen available to mother and baby will be greater, so that both will be less likely to be distressed.

Secondly, when the mother lies flat on her back, her vagina is at an upward slant towards the front of her body. For the baby to be born, the uterus has to work harder, by shrinking more forcefully on the baby to nudge it up the vagina. It is similar to climbing up a mountain. When the mother is upright, on the other hand, the bady has a downward descent, like going down a slide. This downward descent becomes speedier by virtue of the baby's body weight. In 1868 it was calculated that the weight of a full term baby was enough to supply much of the force needed to expel it, provided the mother was upright. As we are aware, the force of gravity, pulls things down in accordance to their weight. That is, a brick will fall quickly with a thud to the ground by virtue of its weight, whereas a feather will gently float to the ground because it is light in weight. An average Indian full term baby weighs about three kilos, or six pounds. When the mother is upright, it is this weight of the baby that pulls the baby downward through the vagina.

It also puts pressure on the mouth of the womb, encouraging it to open.

Thirdly, as the baby slides down the mother's body, to be born, it exits from the lower end of the mother's pelvic structure. Part of the lower circumference of the mother's pelvic structure comprises of the tail bone. The tail bone is a free and flexible bone which very easily moves out of the way, giving the baby a few extra centimetres to be born, provided the mother is not in any way restricting its movement. Its movement can be free when the mother is in an upright position.

(See Pg. 110 for Precaution)

Interestingly, till modern obstetrics came about and birth went to the hospital, all the world over, birth was always in an upright position. In Asia, women sat up or squatted during birth, in the West birth-stools were used. Three factors contributed to this changes:

(1) King Louis XIV of France wanted to watch his mistress give birth. He had her lie down at the time of birth and this made it fashionable to lie down at birth.

(2) Birth went from the home and the midwife, to the hospital and the doctor.

(3) The use of forceps came about, which required the mother to lie down.

*THE WELL BEING OF THE NEW MOTHER MUST BE ENSURED THROUGH FREE ACCESS OF A CHOSEN MEMBER OF HER FAMILY DURING BIRTH AND THROUGHOUT THE POST NATAL PERIOD. IN ADDITION, THE HEALTH TEAM MUST PROVIDE EMOTIONAL SUPPORT.*

According to the Royal College of Midwives and the Royal College of

Obstetricians and Gynaecologists, UK, the presence of a supportive companion in labour is one of the most effective forms of care in childbirth.

The Midwives Information and Research Service points out, "ten randomised, controlled trails, which included over 3000 women, have examined the impact on a woman's labour, of having the continuous presence of a support person......This person......had received brief preparation on how to support women during labour." The results are remarkably consistent, they show that continuous support is associated with:

• lower use of pharmacological anesthesia and fewer epidurals.

• fewer instrument deliveries (example, forceps).

• fewer Caesarean sections.

• more five minute Apgar scores greater than seven. (That is, more babies were born alert, with a good supply of oxygen).

All these trials which looked at women's preferences found that continuous support is associated with:

• labour being better than expected.

• a more positive overall experience for the woman

There were no negative outcomes associated with 'support in labour'.

\* IMMEDIATE BREASTFEEDING SHOULD BE ENCOURAGED EVEN BEFORE THE MOTHER LEAVES THE DELIVERY ROOM.

When the baby is born to a mother who has not received any drugs like pethidine, calmpose etc. in labour, it is born very alert. If such a baby is placed at the mother's breast, it will start suckling. It brings forth a gush of maternal love in the mother, who might until then be wondering about the odd appearance of her new born. Hence, it is said to encourage bonding.

Suckling at birth also causes a release of oxytocin hormone in the mother which causes the uterus to contract, the placenta to be expelled and haemorrhage to stop.

Apart from the above advantages the baby learns to latch on properly to the breast for feeding and does not need to be coaxed and taught later when milk comes in. Also, the baby gets invaluable colostrum which could be the first immunisation the baby receives. The baby is alert at birth, so it is best to feed within 30 minutes of it.

If you want to breastfeed your baby at birth, you could speak to your doctor about your desire. This would include your desire to avoid sedatives being given to you in labour. If you feel shy or embarrased, do not be so. Remember, for the doctor it is one of the ever so many deliveries. For you and your baby however, it is a unique experience that will be etched in your memorey for a lifetime.

The baby does not need glucose water or artificial milk in the first day or two. The best is to breastfeed the baby only when the baby demands a feed (which initially can be six hours or so) and to feed the baby nothing else. Artificial feeds fill the baby's stomach and prevents suckling at the breast.

Realising the importance of this there is an international effort called the Baby Friendly Hospital Initiative (BFHI). These hospitals as a matter of routine avoid over medicating the mother and encourage breastfeeding at birth and afterwards.

In India, such hospitals are now honoured by UNICEF and a task force of the Indian government, and labelled `Baby Friendly Hospitals'. Names and addresses of such hospitals can be had from BFHI, Indian Medical Association, IMA House, Indraprastha Marg, New Delhi 110 002.

\* OBSTETRIC CARE THAT CRITICISES TECHNOLOGICAL BIRTH CARE AND RESPECTS THE EMOTIONAL, PSYCHOLOGICAL AND SOCIAL ASPECTS OF BIRTH SHOULD BE ENCOURAGED.

Using technology in birth stems from the belief that birth is a medicalised event of tremendous risk. According to Ros Claxton in *Birth Matters*, Unwin Paperbacks, 1986, 'the routine application of medical techniques that occurs in most hospitals creates more problems than it solves. Professor G. L. Kloosterman, the Dutch obstetrician, believes that 80-90 per cent of women are capable of normal deliveries without medical intervention'.

Somewhere along the line, people forget that birth is a normal biological event.

Most of the techniques used at birth have not undergone thorough testing. An interesting fact is that the fetal heart monitor, which is strapped on to the mother's abdomen and requires her to lie on her back, causes fetal distress. That is, it causes abnormal heartbeat of the baby, because, when lying on her back the mother compresses a blood vessel. Now, this machine which was designed to identify fetal distress, is found to be actually causing it, if over-used.

It is interesting to know that, during World War II, there was a tremendous strain on medical facilities and specialist care for pregnancy and birth nearly came to a stop. At this time, for some unexplainable reason, obstetric mortality rates (infant and mother death rates) fell to an unprecented degree. This worldwide phenomena seems to have no explanation. (Source: *'Pursuing the Birth Machine'*, Ace Graphics, 1994, by Dr. M. Wagner, consultant to WHO on Women and Child Health).

*INFORMATION ON BIRTH PRACTICES IN DIFFERENT HOSPITALS, SUCH AS RATES OF CAESAREAN SECTION, SHOULD BE AVAILABLE TO THE PUBLIC.*

This will help the public decide where they want to have their children delivered. They can choose a hospital where the percentage of Caesarean section is low, where the use of routine medications is not the norm, where breastfeeding is encouraged, where they will be allowed a labour companion etc.

* THE INDUCTION OF LABOUR SHOULD BE RESERVED FOR SPECIFIC MEDICAL INDICATIONS. NO REGION SHOULD HAVE RATES OF INDUCED LABOUR HIGHER THAN 10%.

According to Wrigley (1962), it is 'questionable whether the oxytocin drip saved the life of a single baby and it is certain that its employment never made labour more normal or more comfortable for the patient.'

However, induction of labour would be medically required if the mother suffers from high blood pressure, diabetes, kidney problem etc.

If induction of labour is over-used it can lead to the rupture of the uterus and a medical emergency.

Futher, as Sheila Kitzinger writes in her book Freedom and Choices in Childbirth, "Induced labours have disadvantages. They tend to be more painful, so induction starts a process in which powerful pain-killing drugs may have to be given. These in turn slow down labour and may lead to a forceps delivery. Induced labours are more likely than spontaneous labours to end in a Caesarean section".

*ARTIFICIAL EARLY RUPTURE OF MEMBRANES, AS A ROUTINE PROCESS IS NOT JUSTIFIABLE.

Sometimes, doctors may burst the bag of water routinely. What this would do is, speed up the birth process. To do this routinely is not recommended, it could lead to distress of the baby, infection in the mother and/or baby, cord prolapse etc.

The textbook *Common Obstetric Problems*' by Ian Donald says, 'With very few exceptions, intact membranes mean an intact mother and an intact baby.'

*DURING DELIVERY, THE ADMINISTRATION OF ANALGESIC OR ANESTHETIC DRUGS (NOT SPECIFICALLY REQUIRED TO CORRECT OR PREVENT ANY COMPLICATION) SHOULD BE AVOIDED.

Drugs are not beneficial to the baby when the mother is pregnant, neither are they beneficial to the baby when the mother is in labour.

Drugs used in labour pass through the placenta and reach the baby's blood circulation, exerting a similar effect to that which is exerted on the mother. Since the baby receives the same dose as the mother, it becomes a massive overdose for the baby. If the mother recovers from the drug in two hours, the baby could take twenty hours to recover from its effect. After birth the baby may be given an antidote injection to the drug. Some drugs, may remain in the baby's system and strain the baby's immature liver to break down and excrete the drug. This could lead to jaundice in the baby.

Apart from drugs, the discomfort of labour can be reduced in several ways. For instance, if the mother has a warm bath or is soaked in a tub of warm water. The temperture of the water in the tub should be body temperature, that is, $98.4^0$ F. Also, moving about in labour and having a sympathetic caring companion would greatly reduce the 'pain' felt by a woman in labour. Further, a positive attitude, conscious 'breathing' and relaxation by the mother will be of tremendous help.

However, it is not a good feeling to go into a hospital with the thought that you and your partner are going to say 'no' to routine medication or procedures. It is better to discuss your choices in advance with your doctor. You could follow it up with a list of preferences stating your choices. The list of your preferences could be attached by your doctor to your case papers. This would be of great convenience to your doctor and to you. If the nursing home and/ or staff is not equipped to allow you your preferness and choics you could consider a change.

The following is an example of how a list of preferences could be:

1) You would like to have minimum of ultrasound.

2) You wish your partner or support person to be present with you during labour.

3) You wish to be able to move around in labour. (You will lie down for examination and if it is a case of a floating head and the water bag bursts).

4) You do not need to have your water bag broken routinely on admission.

5) You do not wish to have medical intervention until you are informed of its necessity.

6) You would like to hold your baby at birth (see p.186-187).

7) You would like to breastfeed the baby exclusively, and so you would not like the bottle or glucose water to be given to the baby.

8) You would like to keep the baby with you in your room.

9) In case your baby is put in special care after birth you would like to hold your baby and give it expressed breast milk, or feed it directly.

10) You would like to attach your requests to your hospital notes.

11) Put the baby in a tub of warm water after the birth.

12) Would like to be informed of any procedure before it is carried out.

WOLVERHAMPTON
PUBLIC LIBRARIES

242

# Index

## A

Abdominal examination, 26-27
Abortion,
    medical termination of pregnancy, 30
    medicine for, 179
    threatened miscarriage, 101-102
Activities, normal activities in pregnancy, 21
AFP, Alpha Feto Protein test, 23, 30
After childbirth,
    after a Caesarean birth, 7-8
    after a normal birth, 156-161, 165-166
Alcohol, 17, 20, 48-49, 51, 75, 231, 233
Amniocentesis, 29-30
Amniotic fluid, 13-14, 107
Amniotic sac, 13-14, 15, 29, 107-108
Anaemia, 58-59
Anatomy, 10-16
    understand your anatomy, 10-13
Antenatal visits, 21-22

## B

Baby,
    at birth, 150
    first trimester, 13-14
    second trimester, 14-15
    third trimester, 15-16
Baby's head at birth, 150
Baby-friendly hospitals, 186
Backache,
    during pregnancy, 40-42
    during labour, 113-114

worries about producing enough breastmilk, 202-203
Breathing,
    a focus in labour, 121, 147
    as a conditioned reflex in labour, 121, 147
    concentration breathing, 126
    levels to be practiced in labour, 122-125
    not pushing breathing, 126-129
    practices to be used in labour, 121, 147
    pushing breathing, 129-130
Breech baby, iii, 16, 154
Burping baby, 203

## C

Cervix, 11-13, 15, 26, 105, 134
Cleft palate, 225-227
Colostrum, 183, 191, 193-194, 221-222
Comfort sucking by baby when breastfeeding, 188-189
Common problems during pregnancy,
    behavioural changes, 44-45
    conditions requiring special attention, 55-62
    digestive problems, 49-53
    physical changes, 33-44
    urinary tract infection, 53-55
Confirming pregnancy, 17
Constipation and piles, 52-53
Contraception after childbirth, 168-179
Contraception in the future, 179
Contractions, 6, 105-107, 111-114, 118, 120-121
Cooking, best methods of, 69
Cow's milk, for baby, 212
Cravings, 44
Cystitis, 53-54

## D

Darkening and pigmentation, 33
Diahorrhea,

of labour, 1-2
    fear tension pain syndrome, 119-120
Flat nipples, 185
Floating head, 110
Food, *see 'Diet'*

## G

Genetic counselling, 20

## H

HCG, human chorionic gonadotropin hormone, 17
Heartburn, 51
HIV drugs,
    azt, 25, 26
    nevirapine, 25-26
    3tc, 25
HIV, percentage of babies that can be affected, 25
Home remedies for,
    anemia, 59
    dental problems, 35
    diarrhoea, 53
    nausea, 49-50
    oedema, 43
    sore nipples, 217
Homoeopathy, 167
Hormones, 17, 156, 167, 210
    endorphins, 146
    oxytocin hormones, 193
    prolactin hormones, 209-210
    relaxing hormones, 156-157
Household chores after childbirth, 157-159

## I

Immunities,
    from breastmilk, to baby, 180-181, 194, 208-209

from mother, 25
Immunoglobin Anti D injection, 21, 60, 142, 223
Infection prevention after childbirth, 156
Itching, 38-39

## J

Jaundice, 222-225

## K

Kesaree, Nirmala, 185

## L

Labour,
        backache in, 113-114, 116-118
        eating during, 73-74
        fear of, 1-2
        first stage, 143-145
        induced, 132-138
        muscle action in, 4-5, 119
        positions to adopt, 109-115, 236-237
        reasons for inducing, 138-142, 240-241
        second stage, 145, 148
        starting signs, 105-108
        third stage, 148-150
Laing, R.D., 152
Leboyer, Fredrick, 152-153
Leg cramps, 36-37
Lifting heavy objects, 20-21
Lightening, 16
Luthra, Meera, 228-330

## M

Mastitis, 219-221
Mature milk, 194-195